MW01119912

I WILL NEVER LEAVE YOU NOR FORSAKE YOU

RONALD W. KNOTT

PublishAmerica
Baltimore

First printing

PublishAmerica has allowed this work to remain exactly as the author intended, verbatim, without editorial input.

Softcover 9781627096454
PUBLISHED BY PUBLISHAMERICA, LLLP
www.publishamerica.com
Baltimore

Printed in the United States of America

"This work is dedicated to anyone who has made Jesus Christ their personal Savior and Lord. In mind was the furtherance of this relationship with Him, over all other things in such a person's life. May you find this work helpful in accomplishing that critical end."

INTRODUCTION

The arrangements for this book are progressive in nature. While there was initial concern for the level of spirituality or degree of relationship the reader may have with the Lord it became quite apparent that it was to be no longer a concern. What we don't know or understand we can seek and/or wait for, because hopefully, we have a hungry heart. Jesus desires to assist us in all of these particular arrangements.

The progression aspect goes from the beginning (**faith**) to (**provision**) to (**works**) and on to the results of the three, comprising of **character**, the **two wills** of God, (**perfect will** and the **will allowed**) and finally the acquisition of **more faith** because of the working of any or all of these aspects. Faith can often beget more faith through obedience from works coming from provisions being given by God. All this is driven by a heart that is being bent toward the Lord.

The focus in the beginning is obviously on faith. Faith is not just a requirement it is **the necessary element** for a relationship with God, whether it is a good one or bad one. When a person begins to acknowledge the existence of God, he or she is responding to a prompting by the Holy Spirit through faith that has been or is in a greater way being imparted to that individual. It is very personal. So personal in fact, that you can look foolish, trying to convince others of what only you can now see. However, if you get in the presence of another person who has been given the same (revelation) there may be a sigh of relief. The other world of unbelief though, is taxing and tiring, just being in its presence. Jesus experienced this and had to get alone with our heavenly Father. There were of course other reasons as well but this principle still has never changed. The Lord desires to bring us to higher ground where wisdom, knowledge, and discernment are established in our hearts. These gifts are going to give decision making new life in all things. These aspects of God are also going to increase as He receives our ongoing cooperation in his often mysterious plan for our lives. We gravitate to higher ground, become more mature or grow in God. The word 'gravitate' is used here because very often we discover we have grown a bit…after the fact. He brought us there but we participated in the divine plan as He aids us in the journey. In effect, we obey Him without conscious thought of growth or reward.

In order to exhibit faith we will come to the subject of God's **Provision**. The means necessary to carry out what He has in mind demands that those critical components of the Lord be there at some point along the way to accomplish what He intends. We will discuss the fact that this subject has one of the highest rankings of building faith in the Christian. Paul mentions the presence of or the lack of provision. The Lord giving, withholding, or taking away provision is vastly covered in examples given for our growth throughout both the Old and New Testaments. We will cover in several forms the subjects of expectation, assumption, presumption, and on the other hand patience, trust, and gratefulness.

"It is better to learn obedience by the things we suffer than to disobey and suffer...and then maybe learn." RWK

The third and final subject is the fruit of all **works**, both inwardly and outwardly. 'Character' is to the man or woman what paint is to canvas. The paint isn't just a superficial substance that gives us a picture. Paint becomes one with the surface, penetrating deep into the fabric and setting a concrete portrayal of what image the artist had in mind to project.

Building character is an ongoing process acquired by submitting to the Lord our hearts and letting Him have his way. During this process His character begins to invade us (the canvas) and his image begins to take shape for other people to see and experience. Believers and unbelievers alike will respond to whatever quality of this character they are presented with. Don't be as concerned about your character. Be as concerned about the obedience issue, focus primarily on the Lord and the character the Lord desires to impart will be there. With respect to constantly monitoring God's progress, be mindful this may become nothing less than a distraction. It may be helpful at times but not making it number one is productive.

As we travel along this life of faith we will be called upon to demonstrate or live out what God has worked in. We will be able to see for ourselves as well, what the Lord was not able to work in as a result of sin, disobedience, or a multitude of hindrances. The revelation of anything most often is accompanied with grace for those who are really open to the Lord's promptings and will respond to his willful purpose for their lives. Provision also has its place here as in any other aspect of the journey.

Each topic has the potential to be a vehicle in which faith is built. In would be good to keep in mind that since everything other than God was created by Him it is also something that may be used as a tool to get something to you. That means anything. Much of that depends on us.

It would not be fitting to have a serious discussion about and with God without bringing the arch enemy of our souls into the picture. Satan, temptation, sin, stumbling and falling are unfortunately still a part of this world in its present state. To fear God and shun evil indelibly makes a man or woman of God a potential subject for these characteristics. Remember this; Satan did not bring up Job…the Lord did. The **Two Wills** of God are used at His discretion as He sees fit. Our discussion about these aspects can create more questions than answers if left unchecked. A heart for God will be poised for truth and then the Lord's discernment will aid and filter out any misconceptions.

Let us take the better path and live a life with Him getting the victory for us because we became His friends His way, and not our idea of His way. As Christians we must operate with full knowledge of the spirit vs. the natural. In *Matthew 28:20* NIV Jesus said;

"And surely I am with you always, to the very end of the age"…

...then He left. Let not this be a discouragement but an encouragement.

The last subject being "**works**" is appropriately located because faith and provision have been sufficiently acquired. The works that we do as Christians will be under the direction and power of God, even the seemingly insignificant or mundane things we do in God. Everything we do, matters to the Lord. The relationship strengthens and benefits others. In the process the Lord expands our horizon and becomes pleased with a son or daughter that obeys what he or she has been given. At the end of this life we may confidently say, "It is finished" and He can say, "Well done good and faithful servant."

Revelation is rightly defined by Webster as "something that is revealed by God to humans" or "an act of revealing or communicating divine truth." Though it may seem to be simple or elementary, the current given state of the church does demand these reminders. Some are 'witnessing' to the world under the guise of revelation but the life doesn't show it. A young Christian may initially not get this due to misunderstanding but may ultimately grow out of it. The heart will always be the weight hanging in the balance of God. *1 Samuel 16:7 NIV*

Man looks at the outward appearance but God looks at the heart.

A revelation of what revelation is, can be cleansing and bring one back on the right track. Misunderstanding or mistaking a revelation from God for a counterfeit is in affect a product of a person's heart, depending on the depth of the 'illumination'. Like faith, revelation is a key element imparted by the Lord to whomever and whenever he chooses. Even unbelievers are recipients of revelation from God. How else do we get saved?

FAITH

In Hebrews chapter 11 also known as the 'faith' chapter the classic biblical definition is laid out from the beginning. Verse 1 in the NIV states:

Now Faith is being sure of what we hope for and certain of what we do not see.

The King James Version puts it:

Now faith is the substance of things hoped for, the evidence of things not seen.

In the footnotes of both versions there are allusions to faith being a vehicle and the works being evidence of faith but the faith aspect is not described as it is written. Faith really is a 'substance'. The Greek word **hypostasis,** meaning 'substance' is not separated from faith. Let's go back to the beginning to see what the Lord did when He created man.

In Genesis 2:7 KJV it reads;

And the Lord God formed man of the dust of the ground and <u>breathed</u> into his nostrils the breath of life; and man became a living soul. 5301 Hebrew

This was the final recorded act of the creation of man. Everything else became a manifestation of this relationship made and subsequently initiated by the Lord. He created man and woman and followed by telling them what he gave them, ultimately voicing the directives which would cause that relationship to remain intact. With Jesus and a couple of **exceptions** written in scripture, everyone else created from that point on was born of a woman uniting with a man thus creating another person.

God's ordained order here was never meant to be out of order.

The conversation between perhaps the three members of the Trinity prior to the creation of man was in its own way, audible in the spirit world. Now there would be the necessity of God having discussion with someone in the physical world before the fall. Gen 1:28 begins a one way conversation from God to Adam. The Lord spoke…Adam listened. We know he heard the Lord because his accountability became apparent when he ultimately ate of the tree and was reminded of it. Later the Lord walked in the garden. Gen 3:11b says:

And he said, Who told thee that thou wast naked? Hast thou eaten of the tree, whereof I commanded thee that thou shouldest not eat? KJV

As the story goes, he blames the woman and the woman blames the serpent in Gen 3:9-13 KJV. Even though there may have been physical presence of God before and after the fall the relationship was now different. The nature of what God created had been altered. Sin entered this world and forced God's hand to use the substance **to a degree** he had not intended before the fall, faith. Now everyone created has a measure of faith deposited in them from birth. It is not to say Adam and Eve didn't. It is clear that the human race was switched onto a different track other than one God wanted. Plan B had to take affect from that point on. By his love he does everything he would have, except it is not available in the same way it was before the fall. That point hurts me. My soul cries out at times to see Him face to face, because sometimes this new life of 'faith and not by sight' just doesn't seem good enough to me. I am like a baby crying for his father.

King David spoke this desire in Psalm 42: 2a

My soul thirsteth for God, for the living God. KJV

In his youth David made a decision. He sought out the Lord in response to the Lord seeking him out. Knocking on the door of one's heart is not just a sentimental analogy of God reaching down to a person, he really knocks on the door of the heart. The response of the person to that knock is what sets the committed apart from the non-committed. It is a shadow of how we operate here in the natural world. A naturally supernatural request of a committed soul to the one true living God is that it will want judged right out of the essence of its sinful state. King David made it clear he wanted the Lord to judge him, over and over again.

Paul the Apostle states in the 11th chapter of 1st Corinthians verse 28a:

But let a man examine himself. KJV

And in verse 31 he states:

For if we would judge ourselves we would not be judged.

A relationship has been established whereby we are moved to keep ourselves spiritually fit by taking stock of ourselves to participate in the joint effort between the God who made us and ourselves. This is done with the substance of faith. It is not just a belief, it is something we have that we cannot prove we have whenever we want. It is still very personal. Although the reference in verse 28 refers to the Lord's Supper, it applies all the time. The nature of this will change back to its original state in heaven for us.

Both examples of David and Paul, the Old and New Testaments respectively are reputations of two individuals who responded to God at different points in their lives, David sooner, Paul later. The point being made is one of saying *"yes Lord, I will follow you wherever you go"*. David needed and got mercy. He pleaded many times for it while Paul needed and got grace.

Psalm 31:9

Have mercy upon me, O Lord, for I am in trouble: mine eye is consumed with grief, yea, my soul and belly. KJV

Paul asked the Lord thrice to remove his thorn in the flesh. The Lord responded in 2 Cor. 12:9

My grace is sufficient for thee: for my strength is made perfect in weakness. KJV

Something happened between the times of these two men. The nature of faith revealed in the Old Testament was different than in the New. The Holy Spirit was in and on men of old but after Jesus came, he left, and sent the Holy Spirit (comforter). God changed the nature of the commands regarding how a relationship was going to be established with him. The spirit came into us in a new way, giving *newness of life.*

When the Lord comes knocking on the door of your heart he does one thing after another before this new relationship is established.

1. Lets me know that I am a sinner and am lost, without remedy from this world.
2. Lets me know that I cannot earn my way to heaven.
3. Lets me know that I knew the whole time He existed even though I knew little about Him. (This is not condemnation, it is conviction continuing) Even people in the bush know of him in the way they do. Jesus has them covered in His own judgements.
4. The knowledge of Jesus being the way back to the heart of God is the only way. He says it in John 14:6

I am the way, the truth, and the life: no man cometh to the father but by me. NIV

If the response from a person is favorable toward the Lord he will now be poised to build faith upon faith, the faith which he initially built into us to respond to Him when he comes calling.

Important Note: If you are already a Christian this may seem redundant or elementary. It is brought up because it is at this point an excess of Christians have gone back, backslidden, or are simply trying to get by with little commitment to God. It hurts, it shows, and has hurt others while most importantly... it grieves God. Return to your first love. Revelation 2:4 states:

Nevertheless I have somewhat against thee, because thou hast left thy first love. KJV

One of the great evidences among us, especially (and shamefully) in clear view of the world is **presumptuous** sins. These are referred to in both the Old and New Testaments. *Numbers 14:44-45 NIV says:*

"Nevertheless, in their presumption they went up toward the high hill country, though neither Moses nor the ark of the Lord's covenant moved from the camp. Then the Amalekites and Canaanites who lived in that hill country came down and attacked them and beat them down all the way to Hormah.

The King James uses 'presumed' instead of 'presumption'. Both words are directly defined as 6075 Hebrew, To swell, to be elated. *Psalm 19:13* uses 'presumptuous'.

"Keep back thy servant also from presumptuous sins; let them not have dominion over me: then shall I be upright, and I shall be innocent from the great transgression". KJV

This denotes arrogance or being proud. (Study; name examples of when David acted in a presumptuous manner?) *2Peter 2:9,10* takes this word a step further.

"The Lord knows how to deliver the godly out of temptations, and to reserve the unjust unto the day of judgment to be punished: but chiefly them that walk after the flesh in the lust of uncleanness and despise government. Presumptuous are they, self willed, they are not afraid to speak evil of dignities." KJV

It would be great if these principle warnings applied only to unbelievers. There is this bold and daring attitude to speak evil of dignities prevailing in the church. Anyone running for or holding a political position is open to unjust cynicism from certain brethren who boldly take it upon themselves to say things that misrepresent God who saved them. The former meaning has to do with a believer that may get blessed by God with something that is used to puff up one's confidence and sometimes move away from God in the thinking that what you are now doing has the stamp of God on it when it actually doesn't. The latter meaning is outright defiance and ignoring any conviction that we are going down the wrong path. Both ends however result in punishment or destruction of some sort. The first meaning may even be a good intention but the second one is a knowing, deliberate act. Not only businesses and human relationships have fallen victim to this line of thinking but entire churches and denominations have been created or destroyed from this error and are going to be judged.

It is time for the truly hungry saints to move on. The hearts' fires have been kindled and the Lord desires to feed His sheep. They hear his voice and follow him wherever he goes.

The big questions remain for the Christian. Is the ground now fit for the Lord to come in and do his work in us regarding the building of faith upon faith? Do we have that desire to know **Him and His ways**?

The old story about the man who said "the big one that got away" almost always refers to a big fish story. One person sees something that no one else saw and is in a perfect position to lie about it or be frustrated because no one else witnessed this exceptional and potential catch. Other possibilities may include a wrong observation or maybe the fishing trip never existed in the first place.

Faith is likened unto the fish story. Only you can witness it for yourself. No one can witness it for you. Even in the upper room where the Holy Spirit came in like a rushing wind in *Acts 2:3*

*came to rest on **each** of them. NIV*

They were all together but experienced it individually. God drives this point home when the areas of accountability come into play. We are judged for what we know, and for what we do not know and should have. It can be a trip up for the brother or sister who may think even for the moment someone else should understand when they may have not heard from God for themselves. A spouse can easily fall into this trap. After a few bouts with rejection or pain resulting from disagreements arising out of not understanding this principle, the Christian may be brought to the place where he or she will now settle down and listen to the Lord more acutely for themselves. (There is also a rejection of truth that does not come from this principle). We'll discuss these aspects later.

Jesus mentions several times in the gospels about the lack of faith in the disciples. Sometimes it even seemed taunting. Four times in Matthews gospel He refers to

"O ye of little faith" KJV

in one form or another. *Matt. 6:30, 8:26, 14:31, 16:8.* His position on their lack was one of care for their spiritual welfare. What Jesus' concern was, the father's concern was.

John 5:19NIV says; "I tell you the truth, the Son can do nothing by himself; he can only do what he sees the father doing, because whatever the father does the Son does also".

He cares for our spiritual welfare as well.

A tool used by the Lord to move in the direction of increasing **faith** is one of pointing out the degree of faith in others, whether it be, a lack or abundance. Either condition can prod one to look at his/her own life and be open to an immediate delivery of more faith from the Father or it may be a gradual impartation at His discretion. The heart determines that course, very often. In Mark 12:43 Jesus in observing a widow's giving at the temple said;

I tell you the truth, this poor widow has put more into the treasury than all the others. They all gave out of their wealth; but she, out of her poverty, put in everything—all she had to live on." NIV

This was and is intended to examine the heart of ones self. Whatever condition the heart is in will determine the quality of faith that will be given. I cannot fool God with anything. How many people enjoy at tax time, the luxury of being given a standard deduction of thousands of dollars and still lie about giving, to the IRS, an arm of the government that Jesus carries on His shoulders. KJV *Isaiah 9:6*—

"For unto us a child is born, unto us a child is given, and the government will be upon His shoulder."

The reading of scriptures can increase faith due a receptive heart being open to what God is speaking to it while being poised or waiting for the bread from heaven. This may be little understood. The mechanics of this will be made known as time and growth permits. The Lord accents this principle in *Luke 8:15 KJV*

"But that on the good ground are they, which in an honest and good heart, having heard the word, keep it, and bring forth fruit with <u>patience</u>.

5281 Greek. '<u>Hupomone</u>'—<u>constancy, waiting, enduring</u>. Spirit begets spirit just like flesh begets flesh. If we with patience do what the Lord expects of us now we will reap more of what and who God is, into our lives. The invasion of God by invitation brings the believer into a more mature state. This principle may also cause many joys and sorrows. *Isaiah 53:3a says;*

"He is* despised and rejected of men; a man of sorrows".
KJV NIV* (was)

However, *Psalm 30:5b* echoes comfort for us.

"Weeping may endure for a night, but joy cometh in the morning". KJV

7440 Hebrew. Cry, gladness, joy, proclamation, rejoicing, shouting, singing, triumph. Some people's morning may be a split second after sorrow is experienced, while another's morning may be the passing of this life into the next. In Luke 16:25 using Abraham in his parable, Jesus mentions the two extremes.

"But Abraham replied, 'Son, remember that in your lifetime you received your good things, while Lazarus received bad things, but now he is comforted here and you are in agony." NIV

Have you ever experienced a moment of sorrow followed by a joy? The long term patience required to last until some mornings is given by God to those he chooses for the longer wait. Again, the heart can determine this action by God. There is a pattern, there is no pattern. A person with a bad heart can get something from God he does not deserve (also in the natural) while someone with a good heart can be denied. This subject of provision will be discussed in the later chapter. There will be times in which God will give you or me something and not a word is to be breathed about it. Patience very often is one of those impartations. Its outworking is only to be observed by others and can be a great instrument to help a struggling or hungry soul in many ways. The Lord watches a response to His demonstration through the other person and depending on the soil's condition may plant a seed, water a seed, or get an increase because some elements were ready to multiply. It is always important however, to desire Him above even the good things he may give spiritually. This desire is the mark of great increase in Him and will be evidenced in a person's life. I saw a man once, exhibit great patience. When I thought he should have spoke or acted, he showed God given restraint. Of course God was watching me as well. I wanted what that man had for patience sake and not God's sake. I had to travel a path perhaps in the same manner that man had, to get more patience than I had in my life. Of course it was painful and I began to realize that quality is one that must be realized as given by the Lord in His time and his way. I can confess I was very late too often in giving God a correct response, thus delaying time and again, growth and knowing Him better as a result.

Faith can be construed as a form of unconscious patience. When we wait for God about anything, He keeps or supplies what is necessary for us to carry on while we wait. And we may not know we are waiting. In *1 Peter 1:5a* referring to the saints he writes;

"who are kept by the power of God through faith" KJV

5432 Greek phroureo—to be a watcher in advance, to hem in, protect. In God's sustaining power he **keeps** us while we wait or endure what it is we are going through. One of the most famous examples of God's 'keeping' power is the story of the burning bush.

Exodus 3:2 And the angel of the Lord appeared unto him in a flame of fire out of the midst of a bush: and he looked, and, behold, the bush burned with fire, and the bush was not consumed. KJV

And the great example in the sight of King Nebuchadnezzar was the three children of Israel being sustained or kept by God in perhaps one of the most dramatic displays of one thing that should have happened and did not. *Daniel 3:23-25 KJV* says:

And these three men, Shadrach, Meshach, and Abednego, fell down bound into the midst of the burning fiery furnace. Then Nebuchadnezzar the king was astonished, and rose up in haste, and spake, and said unto his counselors, Did not we cast three men bound into the midst of the fire? They answered and said unto the king, True, O king. He answered and said, Lo, I see four men loose, walking in the midst of the fire, and they have not hurt; and the form of the fourth is like the Son of God.

While there is much in the translation of some of the words in these scriptures the exhibition of God to an obstinate king is still obvious. The king's response to this display of his power? One of marked change evidenced by this proclamation. Verse 29 accents the king's changed heart.

"Therefore I make a decree, That every people, nation, and language, which speak any thing amiss against the God of Shadrach, Meshach, and Abednego, shall be cut in pieces, and their houses shall be made a dunghill: because there is no other God that can deliver after this sort".

The Lord had something planted in the kings heart that made it possible to get the increase, in this case there was more to come in the king's life which would further God's Glory. Other people's faith can be used to help those even living in the most vile sense. God is always looking for one to step up and say *"Here am I"*. A heart like that pleases Him when it is birthed with His prompting. No agenda, no plans, no ulterior motives that question sincerity, just showing up when He calls. We might not know much about anything, but what really counts is that we approach God with our whole (maybe battered) heart.

"Knowledge can wait…obedience cannot". Pastor Kenneth Marshall*

Whether or not we are aware of it, the leading of God should be the only one. Being consciously aware of his leading in anything is not the rule it is the exception. He means for us to grow out of the need to 'see with our eyes' all the time, evidence that we are on the right track. This is, after all, supposed to be a life of faith. When I first received the Lord into my heart back in 1983 I sought the Lord and His direction whenever I was awake. I needed confirmation, either a physical sign or an event that confirmed I was on the right track. It seemed to work but it was slowly discovered that God was backing off in that type of help for me and 'attempting' to give me faith to trust him. When it came time to move on without all the flashing lights and billboards with direction coming down from heaven, I actually, in my many frustrations still demanded the billboards.

In *Psalm 22* David starts out by saying what our Lord would say later on the cross.

"My God, my God, why have you forsaken me?"NIV

In the very next *Psalm (23)* the king comes back around and proclaims;

"The Lord is my shepherd; I shall not want."

Much happened between the first verses of each Psalm. David expressed what was going on in his heart to God. The Lord did not forsake him, it only seemed like it. Telling God anything is not new to him. It is good for our soul to say it even though the one we are talking to already knows it. He rewards our effort by imparting life for death. Coming to the end of myself brings me to the beginning of a new work from God. The exchange of humility and expression of it to God, for a portion of His faith is the best deal any Christian could have. And of course, that precious principle cannot be abused because God will not be fooled by a heart that does not really seek him. He will make adjustments as he sees fit.

*Psalm 37: 3-5 says; "**Trust** in the Lord, and do good; so shalt thou dwell in the land, and verily thou shalt be fed. **Delight** thyself also in the Lord; and he shall give thee the* *desires of thine heart.* **Commit** *thy way unto the Lord; trust also in him; and he shall bring it to pass."* KJV

Trust, delight, and committing **in him** are not just 'a key' but 'the key'.

This brings us to another important aspect of faith. What do I do to redeem the time? Paul says in *Ephesians 5:15-16 KJV*

"See then that you walk circumspectly, not as fools, but as wise, **redeeming** *the time because the days are evil".*

The word redeeming in this use means *'exagorazo'* 1805 Greek—'to buy up, ransom, to rescue from loss.' In the business world there is an assigned value to time. The quote "time means money" comes to mind. There is an inherent value placed on time, particularly if there has been an assigned limit to it. Our time here has an assigned limit. The maximum time currently is 120 years, a significant number in the bible, and for many throughout the generations even that limit has been cut short. Now that I have the Lord in my life what am I doing with the time I have now come to realize he is giving me? If I am yoked with Him, the time I spend is the time He spends because we are yoked together and then nothing is lost. The original Greek meaning suggests there is something about the nature of time in my life that can be rescued. Sin cut short the natural essence of time in the human life but Jesus came to not just save us but give us life as we redeem the time. This 'time' which originally would have been forever, now has a limitation thrust upon it by the sinful state. We had to have a way back to the heart of God and Jesus Christ was assigned the task of redeeming us from loss. When I accept that condition I enter into the world that has always existed and now works from the principles of that world. If I choose not to, that is where there is loss.

As we move on in God the amount of his ministry increases in us. All of a sudden that which was always there, now becomes alive by the spirit of the Lord. The animal kingdom, the stars, and things in the world of science, etc. etc. will now become living examples of the knowledge of him. Recently discovered animal life near the bottom of the ocean is interesting at the least to just about anyone. The shapes, sizes, colors and behavior of each of the species will dominate the studies of many professionals to the enjoyment of all of us.

To the person who knows God though, this new knowledge can take on a different light. For example, one of the new animals discovered in total darkness, miles down in the sea, deals with an enemy in a way we as humans do. It looks something like a small squid and when chased by the fish that wants to eat it (both which are lit by something called bioluminescence material) this creature shoots out an ink like substance that when it gets a distance away from itself the ink explodes into a bright light display thus distracting the fish away from squid like creature. What is further interesting about this principle it that we use this concept in aviation. A jet when being chased by either another enemy jet or encounters a missile attack either from the air or ground it uses what the squid like creature uses. These are called countermeasures. A material or object is dropped or fired into the air to distract the heat seeking missile away from its intended target. In the natural world, there are many things that may be interesting to the senses. Those things we can see with our naked eye either live or in photography. The other senses of hearing, taste, smell, and touch can be also tantalized by much of what God has created.

The knowledge of God goes beyond mere observation through the senses. Remember, this is a life of faith, not sight. Paul starkly reminds us of this when referring to this ongoing and developing relationship with God. In *Romans 14:19-22* the apostle speaks about doing anything which would cause a brother to fall.

"Let us therefore make every effort to do what leads to peace and mutual edification. Do not destroy the work of God for the sake of food. All food is clean, but it is wrong for a man to eat anything that causes someone else to stumble. It is better not to eat meat or drink wine or do anything else that would cause your brother to fall. So whatever you believe about these things keep between yourself and God. Blessed is the man who does not condemn himself by what he approves." NIV

He punctuates the point by saying something we may have taken very lightly. Verse 23 concludes the chapter by saying,

"But the man who has doubts is condemned if he eats, because his eating is not from faith; and everything that does not come from faith is sin."

What does all of this have to do with squid and jets?

What happens is that as a Christian becomes yoked with the Lord, God is now in a position to reveal Himself to that person through the examples in the natural world in a new way. He could not, prior to that, because of existing conditions in the individual, not because of himself. Oh, how we have made a fetish of everything God has created. Each of those things has become gods and we go to great lengths to protect them, all because we have not sought the one who made them. It is amazing the new groups and societies that have been formed and dedicated to things so miniscule or insignificant. When God illuminates them though, what was insignificant now is as big as God because He is in it. What lessons can we learn about God? What better relationship can I have with the Lord when I see an animal squirt out a countermeasure against an attack in darkness? That depends on my relationship I currently have with Him.

So whatever you believe about these things keep between yourself and God. V.22a

The Lord never changes…He just reveals more of himself.

Doubt is the antipode of faith. Doubt is not to be confused with simply 'not knowing' or 'not understanding'. Throughout the Old Testament the people were reminded of the presence of doubt in their lives, both as individuals and as a group. In many stories we read where there is even the appearance of strong dedication and commitment to a person, principle, or cause but as we read on further, the real state of that person or people is revealed. It is important to discuss doubt in a Godly portion because the Lord gives us examples bountifully as to what not to do. Of course we are not to make an unreasonable discourse about it.

In *Job chapter 2:12,13* Job is addressed by three friends. The men display that commitment and patience, much needed to do what they did. Starting in verse 12 is an act of just how much they were affected by observing Job's condition.

*"When they **saw** him from a distance, they could hardly recognize him; they began to weep aloud, and they tore their robes and sprinkled dust on their heads." NIV*

Then came the impressive work of patience by the three men. Verse 13 states;

*"Then they sat on the ground with him for seven days and seven nights. No one said a word to him, because they **saw** how great his suffering was."*

No matter what happens in this natural world, no matter what it is we see with our eyes, unless the Lord brings it home and alive to us we are only affected in the flesh for a season. In some way I can be affected even for the rest of my life, by something I see naturally. The nature of the affect and its remembrance is what God wants control of in our lives. The children of Israel went through the Red Sea on dry ground but its affect was short lived because of the heart conditions of the people. Time after time God came to them before and after the Exodus with great miracles.

God's approach to us will reveal what the heart condition is. His ministry will fit exactly what the state of my heart is. He knows me much better than I do, whether I think something is too little or too much. How is the heart to be softened? How can I change? The same way it gets hardened. By God. The

Lord himself takes the credit for everything. *Exodus 7:3* the Lord speaks;

"But I will harden Pharaoh's heart, and though I multiply my miraculous signs and wonders in Egypt, he will not listen to you." NIV

When a heart is hard, even a person's response and call to action does not mean that the heart was softened. Contrary to its appearance, our heart can recoil into a deeper hardness than before because of its self seeking effort to stay alive. The faith of God, given to us, will take care of the belief I have about what it is He does. Paul says in *Philippians 4:11-12 KJV*

"Not that I speak in respect of want: for I have learned, in whatsoever state I am, therewith to be content. I know both how to be abased, and I know how to abound: everywhere and in all things I am instructed both to be full and to be hungry, both to abound and to suffer need".

How did Paul get this way? A man, who notoriously persecuted the church approving even to the death of some, now carries in him the fuller life of our Lord Jesus. A willing heart that responds to the Lord Himself by this humbling submission creates the opening whereby God comes in, thus adding or building upon himself in residence of the believer. The principle is found in everyday life. You really do reap what you sow. Just because many people do not see the manifestation of the Lord's work in you and I right now, does not mean it isn't happening. We determine a lot more than we know by the decisions we make in our hearts and minds.

Many years ago I was in tremendous emotional pain. I lay in bed at night wishing the unavoidable trauma of the loss of a loved one to just go away. An angel from the Lord came and stood in my doorway. I had been facing away from him and sensing the presence in the room, I was afraid to turn around, but did. Although I still had doubts about what I was going to see, he really was there, saying not a word. I could not look him in the face but squinting away a tear from my eye, a peace from the Lord came and comforted me in my pain. I turned around and in facing the wall again went comfortably to sleep. This experience did not seem at all to mature me into a greater faith. It was just an experience, albeit a great one. We've all had them in one sense or another. What I did learn was that God did not require me to be spit polished and wearing clean fine white linen before he showed up that night. In scripture we see many instances where the Lord sends his angels to people, some of which seemed to qualify because of their righteousness, some because of their unrighteousness, and at times just because God is sovereign. He can do whatever he wants when he wants.

Paul's journey into Christianity began with the presence of the Lord himself to Paul. *Acts 9:1-6* states this dramatic event.

"And Saul, yet breathing out threatenings and slaughter against the disciples of the Lord, went unto the high priest, and desired of him letters to Damascus to the synagogues, that if he found any of this way, whether they were men or women, he might bring them bound to Jerusalem. And as he journeyed, he came near Damascus: and suddenly there shines round about him a light from heaven: And he fell to the earth, and heard a voice saying unto him, Saul, Saul, why persecutest thou me?

And he said, Who art thou Lord, what wilt thou have me to do?
And the Lord said unto him, Arise, and go into the city, and it
shall be told thee what thou must do." KJV

Saul, now named Paul had been doing what he thought was
God's service. We can only speculate what was going on in
his heart with respect to conviction and guilt but his response
to coming to him in this way can make us think that he was a
man who needed exactly what he got. The Lord knew his heart
and ministered accordingly.

The heart captured by God can now be a vessel not only in
which to dwell but to build upon himself, the solid rock. This
response by invitation in a man or woman for God to dwell
in his or her body is the beginning of new life, nurtured by a
continuing invitation, grows and matures us as the Lord now
has something to work with. Faith continues to increase as
the one we invited in now is able to take us places he could
not before. Assisting and sustaining us in all things will make
the growth necessary to get his increase but now can be used
successfully in many areas, *especially* the nourishment of
other people who have the same spirit, and examples to those
who do not.

ANGELS

We are going to delve slightly into an often misunderstood subject, particularly in the believer. It is important to refer back to when Saul heard the voice of the Lord. Those men who were with him did not experience the exact same thing.

Acts 9:7,8 "The men traveling with Saul stood there speechless; they heard the sound but did not see anyone. Saul got up from the ground, but when he opened his eyes he could see nothing. So they led him by the hand into Damascus." NIV

They may have heard something but it is clear they did not understand fully what was going on between the Lord and Saul. They had not fallen to the ground, but stood there speechless. The important point here lies in two aspects. The **intimacy of God** and the **infinite spectrum of angels** he has had here with us the whole time. Both of these primary points are distinctly related to what an angel really is…biblically speaking.

The Hebrew word for 'angel' found in the Old Testament from the books of Genesis through Zechariah is *'malak'* 4397 or in English meaning; **ambassador, angel, king, messenger**.

The entire New Testament from Matthew to Revelation when using angel in the singular form describes it as *'aggelos'* 32 in Greek, meaning **'messenger'** in English.

Throughout the bible there are many instances where angels bring messages to individuals or groups of people. The main understanding of an angel in this sense is our view that these angels have either a human or some heavenly form we just haven't seen yet. But there is more to this. The word messenger in the Old Testament Hebrew is exactly the same as angel, only many of the messengers are not "angelic" angels. They are people. It can be a priest as in *Malachi 2:7*

"For the lips of the priest ought to preserve knowledge and from his mouth men should seek instruction—because he is the **messenger** *of the Lord Almighty."* NIV

A messenger is a carrier of a message from God to a person or persons. The **intimacy of God** begins here.

The love of God to each person is very personal. Individually, every man, woman and child has, is, and will be subject to degrees of the love of God whether they know it or not. Some may not know either through deficit or disobedience but He is still there.

"God is love. Whoever lives in love lives in God, and God in him." *1 John 4:16b*
NIV

This degree is the greatest form of love and for the Christian it is unwavering on God's part. To those who are in God are in love. Jesus said in

Rev. 3:19a "Those whom I love I rebuke and discipline." NIV

How does he rebuke and discipline? As many ways as He has messengers.

Hebrews 11:6b says *"He rewards those who earnestly seek Him."* NIV

How does he reward those who earnestly seek Him? Throughout the bible there are countless examples of God saying he will do this, have done that, or in a more current sense, he is doing it. He covers all three tenses to an individual or more than one person thus the **infinite spectrum of angels/** messengers. The point made is that he uses anyone or anything, good or evil, as a messenger at any time he chooses. God came to Baalam in Numbers 22 by using an angel as a messenger and a donkey as well. Can you imagine having a donkey you are riding turning his head around and starts talking to you? The unfortunate thing for God is we see he has been forced to use too often the external form of messaging. Again, this is supposed to be a walk of faith not one of sight. Even the external form may not bring people to him as he would want. Everything he has created qualifies to be used as a messenger to us. Our heart condition will often dictate what methods or form the Lord will take in his attempt to get a message across.

On September 11th 2001 we all know what happened. Terrorists carried out an evil plot to destroy as many people as they could while taking their own lives as well. The faith of many was tested. It is well known that church attendance nationally skyrocketed right after these horrific events. When the initial effects of that fateful day began to wear off so did the commitment to go to the place of worship for many. It went back to business as usual. Our way of life was disturbed and when the apparent return to it occurs, it is delusional. This worldly aspect has been active in the church.

Exodus chapters 16 and 17 points out the recoiling nature of man, to return to this state of obstinacy or stubbornness. Ex.16:2 reflects the heart of man.

"In the desert the whole community grumbled against Moses and Aaron." NIV

They wanted food. If they needed food God would have given it to them. The people are certainly worth more than the sparrow whom Heavenly Father feeds. The children of Israel's view of their lack, was not the view God wanted them to have. He supplied the manna, the quail, and water from the rock anyway. How far did these acts bring the people? Since he knows what we need before we ask, why ask? "The relationship". A son or daughter should ask because of the relationship, not necessarily because of need or want. It will be a joy to ask the Lord for something when the relationship is right. It enhances the relationship. That is the point in asking. Jesus asked the disciples in Luke 24:41b

"Do you have anything here to eat?" NIV

What a breathtaking question! God asking me for something to eat! My first reaction may be, "I've got to run to the store and get a steak, can you **wait** a few minutes?" Or I may think, "No, he likes fish!" What would really happen if I really knew who I was talking to is to outright weep. What can I offer the God of all creation, a selection from the shelf in my house? **Maybe.** The truth is that all the disobedience of the children of Israel was recorded for us not to follow in their footsteps. May we learn from Him the lessons he intends.

The revelation of **God's character** comes largely in part because we are diligently seeking Him and He reveals himself. When a person begins to know God there is always the risk of thinking we know him in a way we really don't. (Sort of, filling in the blanks when he hasn't revealed those particular aspects yet). What happens after the assumption, is, potential contention with other people. What happened on September 11th? Why did God allow such a thing to happen? If we have passed the initial threshold of knowing the Lord and the love of the Lord...we would know. It is his nature to build up and tear down, to make alive and take the life. After all, he made it. He is the master potter and he can do with these vessels what he wants...and in any way he wants. That means anything, anyone, any way. Nothing is excluded. The holocaust, world wars, a steak dinner, all of it. Good and evil alike. God the Father, Jesus Christ, and the Holy Spirit are responsible for having created everything and they can do with it what they will. Our responsibility is to acknowledge **his** true position on this and when he knocks at the door of our heart, to acknowledge **our** true position in our sinful state. We are not only something he has created but are subsequently damaged by sin. But we are not without remedy. He has made a way for us, not only to come to him humbly, when he calls, but to further submit to him for the provisions meant to sustain us in our walk with Him from that point on.

It was said during a recent documentary that the reason New York City was chosen as the main target was that there was a great Jewish population there. The enemy had plainly declared that America was suffering because of her embracing the state of Israel. What should be more important is what God says about what he did and not voices of the angels he used. It was never about the Jews or the hatred of them. It has been the rebellion of sinful man and his reluctance to come to God when he calls. We just fight amongst ourselves because of the assumptions we have made about God. The wars of this earth today have boiled down to two issues; God and money. I cannot serve both. Matthew 6:24 says:

"No one can serve two masters. Either he will hate the one and love the other, or he will be devoted to the one and despise the other. You cannot serve both God and money." NIV

Assumption and presumption has been turned into a god, just like money.

Christians are not supposed to attempt to reveal God's character and nature verbally on a whim to other people. Either I have been captivated by God and will be directed by him or I won't. I may not be aware of his present workings but a sudden check from the Lord about anything will occur and I then, will not cast my pearls before swine.

Again, what man may have in mind as an end for his intentions may not be what God has in mind. On August 5th, 2004 President George W. Bush had increased his list of well documented blunders by something very profound. Not only did he most likely not know what he was saying, it is clear the mockers did not. On the surface it looks like a big mistake but an ear to hear can pick it up. President Bush had said at the signing ceremony for a defense spending bill: "Our enemies are innovative and resourceful, and so are we. They never stop thinking about new ways to harm our country and our people, and neither do we."

Proverbs 14:12 "There is a way that seems right to a man but in the end it leads to death." NIV

It seems right to not speak of sin during a presidential campaign. It seems right to not mention that sin has anything to do with the need to address the issue of healthcare. The greatest percentage of healthcare dollars are spent on the results of lifestyle choices and the whole nation picks up the tab for it. It is not only our enemies that seek new ways to harm us here in America but we ourselves seek it even more. The manifestation of it lies out in the open for all to see. Then when we try to export our evil practices to countries that have their own set of problems and deplore the immoral and unethical ways of the United States, we resist that notion. The character of God is displayed but not revealed to all. When the towers came down we only saw an enemy do an evil thing, not that maybe, just maybe, the God of heaven and earth was dealing with us about something. God is a jealous God. Money is another god he is jealous of. The various immoral acts that have permeated our society including the church are gods He is jealous of. The World trade Center was the hub for all the economies of the world. It was more than just a symbol, it was built to serve 'mammon' and seven years to the week during September 2008 the stock market fell 777 points. That was the end of the warning. We began a journey unprecedented into economic chaos that continues to this day. The number seven in the bible always means 'completion'. Eight illustrates 'a new beginning'.

What has God provided for us who stand with him in calm and silent humility? Maybe we have our own fleeting thoughts about how something should really be handled?

As we watch the crumbling of the world we must allow ourselves to be taken wherever He wants to take us on the inside. The external events become more of a shadow as one submits to God more and more. The affects of circumstances are not the same anymore as the reality of God's nature come into view and the world becomes *strangely dim*. Hope increases as the Lord who made us exhibits his power by His mere presence. **Provision** now is becoming realized and the relationship is further strengthened. Perhaps the greatest stage for God to work with us is in 'fire'. What angels have you had in your life?

PROVISION

"The fearful and unbelieving world is now full of desperate optimism." RWK

But the saints of God are being prepared for the Lord's ministry to all people in a dark hour. Those who desire what the godly saint has, will be longing for something now hidden, unless by an intercessor it may be released by an act of mercy from the Lord, to a new receptive heart.

Our *God is a consuming fire.*

Provisions in the fires of God

Let it be repeated that the two kinds of trouble have been reduced to mainly one. The trouble I cause myself is at a minimum, and instead of me causing all the turmoil it is now the Lord's turn. He has a tender heart to work with and the beginning of deepest joys and sorrows can now be experienced.

Our current state or condition demands assistance from somewhere else. We must choose where that somewhere is. The selections are many. For every need, there is a solution in one form or another. Our world has been reduced to at times, **trying** to do what God wants, not what the world wants. We are being asked to do many things that only seem insurmountable. Things other than God himself all still clamor for attention as the soothing fix for our problems. Some are quick fixes, while others will demand a lengthy commitment. The problems we face as a Christian now are illuminated as spiritual ones and can only be resolved by the one great spiritual solution, God. What was once seen as a worldly problem could not even be solved by the world. The provisions of the world are dead without God. The same things that are dead will be made alive at his choosing when he feels he can.

When we build anything it must be made with elements (provisions) dispensed by the Lord. The end of any other building is loss. Any other labor is in vain, and this includes us personally. 1Corinthians 3: 10-15 Paul expounds.

*"By the grace God has given me, I laid a foundation as an expert builder, and someone else is building on it. **But each one should be careful how he builds.** For no one can lay any foundation other than the one already laid, which is Jesus Christ. If any man builds on this foundation using gold, silver, costly stones, wood, hay, or straw, his work will be shown for what it is, because the Day will bring it to light. It will be revealed with fire, and the fire will test the quality of each man's work. If what he has built survives, he will receive his reward. If it is burned up; he himself will be saved but only as one escaping through the flames."* NIV

Fire reveals character. God is revealing what I am made of. If we attempt to build what we think is God's character by means other than Him, the character that is built will fail when the trial by fire comes to reveal that character. If he was allowed to build it through a fire, another revealing fire will make known to all what was really used to build it. God made us. He tears things down, recreates and blesses us with his work in us to create his own character. What provisions does he offer us when we have decided to follow him, though none go with me, no turning back, no turning back? First he offers us a chance to repent of our sins as Christians. Repentance is always a gift from God. Worldly sorrow doesn't cut it. When we dry our eyes and start walking humbly with our God he can now start to build into us some of his character. Now the things of the world can be illuminated in the spiritual realm and used by God as tools to build His character. A person who once was a goad through bad character and evil ways now is viewed by me as a provision, not as an unrepentant enemy and someone I don't want any business with. Someone once said; "The devil can only do you good."

We say; "What would Jesus do?" Thinking if we respond the same way he would, maybe has a good intention in it, but it still does not build God's character into us if the Lord was not consulted in the beginning. How do we know this is true? Look around at the character being built and what people are building with. **The character always matches perfectly that which was used to build it.** What is unfortunate for many people is that many things are revealed after the fact and we suffer for it. We discover in frustration that we have avoided God's provision and built nothing of value to Him. It just burns up.

He provides the fire, we provide the sacrifice. *Hebrews 12:29* reads

"for our God is a consuming fire." NIV

He has previously said there are things that will not be burned up. Those things are the things he builds...with His provisions. The heart of the person is the key to all of this. *Psalm 51:17* says what our sacrifices are to be.

"The sacrifices of God are a broken spirit; a broken and contrite heart, oh God you will not despise." NIV

'Sacrifices of God' means those sacrifices that are acceptable to Him. They are 'of Him' because they were gifted to us 'from Him'. No one has ever repented without the gift of repentance 'from Him'. This new state of our heart now becomes an acceptable sacrifice to him. We offer back to him what he gave us. How do we get such a gift...even if we want it and do not presently have it? We will use what he 'has already given'. Patience, love, charity, etc. are now on stage and God is glorified because we have made a decision not to seek the world for our solutions...but Him alone. *He never leaves us without enough provision to carry us wherever he has called us. This applies to how much, where, the timing, all aspects.

*He may also choose to meet us there with those provisions. I may run through the wilderness for forty days on the substance of one meal.

Isaiah 47:15 KJV echoes the truth that these provisions build something that will not be lost.

For this is what the high and lofty One says—he who lives forever, whose name is Holy: "I live in a high and holy place, but also with him who is contrite and lowly in spirit, to revive the spirit of the lowly and to revive the heart of the contrite.

So, everything of value to God in me, about me, is given to me from Him alone. How he gets these things to us is where we can stumble. All things are 'from God' but not all things are not 'of God'. To use a most extreme example is the case of our Lord Jesus, prophesied in *Isaiah 53:6-10a. KJV*

*"We all, like sheep, have gone astray, each of us has turned to his own way, and the Lord has laid on him the iniquity of us all. He was oppressed and afflicted, yet he did not open his mouth; he was led like a lamb to the slaughter, and as a sheep before her shearers is silent, so he did not open his mouth. By oppression and judgment he was taken away. And who can speak of his descendants? For he was cut off from the land of the living; for the transgression of my people he was stricken. He was assigned a grave with the wicked, and with the rich in his death, though he had done no violence, nor was any deceit in his mouth. **Yet it was the Lord's will to crush him and cause him to suffer...**"*

Many sermons and commentaries have been sufficient to cover the circumstances in Jesus's life. He suffered, we suffer. There could be innumerable messages on the elements and functions of suffering. The point always was; is the relationship between the Lord and ourselves such as he can do whatever he wants? Even the way of the cross had provision from heaven. When the world's ways tend to be the measuring stick, Jesus' mission was a failure. But, when a heart has truly surrendered to God, it will always precipitate success, God's definition of success. Jesus had now acquired the answer for all of man's problems, not only the sacrifice for our sins but the path and means to eternal life. Life imparted to the truly faithful. The continuing scripture reference from above reads;

*...and though the lord makes a guilt offering, he will see his offspring and prolong his days, and the **will of the Lord** will prosper in his hand.*

There is great reward for such humble submission to God. You can't fake it. Either the Lord has given it to us or he hasn't. Use what you have in your hand and he will be faithful beyond our imagination. Gifts from the Lord are meant to be used by him in his way.

THE VIRAL COMMUNITY—ASKING FOR AN EARTHLY KING.

Sin is evidence there is a God. The descent into rejecting the one true living God and becoming self reliant started first with Adam and Eve, then corporately, with His chosen people. The heathen nations made their stand without God in their lives, serving other gods. But God chose a people out of all the nations for himself and they refused the call. While there was mass rebellion of all sorts up to the birth of Samuel, the nation of Israel did not actively demand to replace God with a human ruler until 1Samuel chapter 8. **(It is important to note**

**that Samuel was mentioned in *Hebrews 11:32* as possibly
assigned the title of the 'greatest prophet'. Verse 32 says:
"Samuel and the prophets.")** Samuel's sons are interestingly
the one's who participate in the demand to remove God as
King and set up an earthly king. They did not follow the
Lord as their father had. All this is in response to the Lord
reaching out to them, only not in the way they wanted.
There was inconvenience, acquiring money wrongfully and
perverting justice. They were judges appointed by Samuel.
God's **provision** was not enough in their eyes. The way to get
more was to get God out of office and install someone else.
Although God gave ample warning of such actions, he allowed
it when they continually refused to listen to his counsel. From
that point on, the whole world has become saturated with this
kind of walk. Without God, we are without remedy.

When the Lord's approach to us becomes known, there
is given a time to respond. Early on it may not really be
acknowledged that it was God but only 'something to
consider'. God aids us with his provisions contained in that
particular approach. For example; the Lord brings a certain
circumstance into my life. It might be a slow moving line at
the cash register. With a person and a handful of coupons in
front of me and maybe not a care at all about the fact they are
holding me up, I can do one of many things. But not all the
choices are **of** God. What does God provide for me during a
time like that? What is his best? The best is to acknowledge
Him in all my ways. He offers himself to be captivated and to
captivate. That is his best. There are a dozen and one lessons to
be taught about why God may be doing it but my relationship
should always come first…then revelation may come about
the other things. He decides what he wants to share about

what he has done. (He may reveal nothing) There will be no more guessing and trying to live on that guess. That line of thinking always comes to an end. In God there is no end. So his provision at the time is himself. If I am having in His view a good relationship with him, the wait, the whys, and all that my mind can imagine goes by the wayside, right where they belong. The delivery of God with his provisions is right 100% of the time.

Doubt, unbelief, sin, and disobedience may follow a lacking relationship with the Lord. Murmuring and complaining plagued the children of Israel because not only did they not trust him, they simply did not want to wait. His provisions were demanded of him before he ultimately was able to give them. They did not qualify at the time.

Exodus 17:1-2; "The whole Israelite community set out from the Desert of Sin, traveling from place to place as the Lord commanded. They camped at Rephidim, but there was no water for the people to drink. So they quarreled with Moses and said, "Give us water to drink." Moses replied, "Why do you quarrel with me? **Why do you put the Lord to the test?"** KJV

It doesn't matter what we imagine or think, it will always be about the relationship with God. It is an age old problem to seek comfort in what God gives and the personage of God is pushed aside in the process. Comfort in other people, material things, even the unseen spiritual gifts from God to the believer can get exalted to a place higher than God the giver.

*Matthew 6:33 says; "Seek ye **first** the kingdom of God and His righteousness and all these things will be added unto you."* KJV

The relationship between man and God can be developed into one in which any occurrence will only make it better. The same things can make it worse, depending upon the heart of the person. So, it is the Lord we test, not the Moses' or other people in our lives. (We, of course, do affect other people) God is really the one deepest affected by our decisions. He is after the perfect relationship. In *Matthew 5:43-48* Jesus says this point clearly.

"You have heard that it was said, 'Love your neighbor and hate your enemy.' But I tell you: Love your enemies and pray for those who persecute you, that you may be sons of your Father in heaven. He causes his sun to rise on the evil and the good, and sends rain on the righteous and the unrighteous. If you love those who love you, what reward will you get? Are not even the tax collectors doing that? And if you greet only your brothers, what are you doing more then others? Do not even the pagans do that? Be perfect, therefore, as your heavenly father is perfect." NIV

We are incapable of doing these things without the Lord's help. Just because we read these words on the page does not mean we can have these qualities at this time. We may, but only if the Lord gives us them. How do we become perfect as He is perfect? By dying daily, remembering him in all our ways, his impartation to us will be the capstone and we will become perfect as He is perfect. We become His expression. The gates which we operate will let in God and keep out other gods. Our eyes, ears, and mind by choosing Him, will be more and more in control by Him until he invades by invitation, every part of our being.

The consequences of rebellion are not to be a subject spent much time on but those seeking a better relationship may do well to be reminded or learn something new concerning any threats to the salvation and the subsequent growth of our souls.

We as a people have gone astray. We have gone astray from the one who made us. In order to keep the distance from God and at the same time maintain our own flow of provisions there must be a need, a means and a source. This sounds almost like crime, ie, means, motive, and opportunity. In Exodus chapters 7-11 the plagues of Egypt one at a time hardened Pharaoh's heart (the Lord hardened Pharaoh's heart). Each time the Lord came to the king of Egypt through difficult means, the responses ranging from the leader were sounding sincere, to looking sincere, but all fell short of absolute change in looking toward God. If you read one or two stories all the way near the end you could be easily convinced Pharaoh finally got it and swung toward the Lord. Not once did that happen. His response became harsher each time, finally declaring death would be imminent if Moses showed his face again. Remember, it is the Lord that is tested. God is treated as if he is trying to call our bluff on something. Mankind walks blindly toward the end of his life giving little or no thought of the correct responses to the many promptings of God. Therefore man will be without excuse. The track record of God's evidence to such a person and the subsequent refusal of it will be exposed and ready for judgment. This occurs all day and night every moment of our lives. Even silence and no observable evidence is part of God in his ministry to us. What matters is the use of what he has already given and how it is used.

Satan offers many substitutes for God's blessings to his people. Sometimes it may even be exactly the same thing but the timing is off. This may be readily received because of our lust. The mind is near the heart of the matter. **The heart is to the mind what a rudder is to a ship**. James uses a similar principle in another illustration.

James 3:4-6 says: "Or take ships as an example. Although they are so large and are driven by strong winds, they are steered by a very small rudder wherever the pilot wants to go. Likewise the tongue is a small part of the body, but it makes great boasts. Consider what a great forest is set on fire by a small spark. The tongue also is a small fire, a world of evil among the parts of the body. It corrupts the whole person, sets the whole course of his life on fire, and is itself set on fire by hell." NIV

The rudder of a ship though, may be used for selfishness and may lead the entire ship into boisterous seas. The tongue can be controlled **to a degree**. The world takes pride in this kind of control. The problem though is this. It produces more of its own kind. There are many people, including preachers, multiplying themselves through firstly what is in their heart, and then what comes out of their mouths. This principle has to have hearts receptive to the message being spoken. (Weight loss programs and the like all have their success stories. Anyone who determines to be a part of something can make that cause look successful) That will depend on the heart condition of the speaker and the hearer. A heart bent on knowing God, will have the benefits from allowing Him to be directly involved in the filtering (discernment) process. A heart bent on things other than knowing Him, will be open for error, and the satisfactions of desire for **created things**. The danger of worsening a state of lust, especially in today's world, has created grave concern.

Many viruses have been discovered in the laboratory. Depending on their nature and what they do to man, the search for something that will stifle or eliminate a particular strain is sought unknowingly in vain. New advances in antiviral antibodies are hailed as the answer to the problem. Some strains have actually been eliminated. There are samples of certain strains that have been eradicated from the mainstream human population that are still under lock and key. There are others that mutated because of the use of such antibodies. These have become resistant to any known antibodies and are a threat to society. The virus had been exposed to something that posed a threat to its existence and simply altered its defenses to render the medicine which once seemed helpful to a patient, now useless. We can act the same way toward God.

The beginning of the plagues in Egypt signaled the beginning of the trek of approaches by the Lord and the subsequent rejections by the Pharaoh and his counselors. As such exists today, there were also people among the population in Egypt that were mindful of God's principles. Exodus 7 starts God's proclamation that he was going to not only come to Pharaoh and his leaders, but speaks of Himself as the one who hardens Pharaoh's heart, leading to the resistance against the Lord's mighty wonders.

Exodus 7:1-5 *"Then the Lord said to Moses, "See, I have made you like God to Pharaoh, and your brother Aaron will be your prophet, You are to say everything I command you, and your brother Aaron is to tell Pharaoh to let the Israelites go out of his country. But **I will harden Pharaoh's heart**, and though I multiply my miraculous signs and wonders in Egypt, he will not listen to you. Then I will lay my hand on Egypt and with mighty acts of judgment I will bring out my divisions, my people the Israelites. And the Egyptians will know that I am the Lord when I stretch out my hand against Egypt and bring the Israelites out of it." NIV*

Moses gets to hear firsthand who God is when He says; "I will harden Pharaoh's heart." Still, with us it is the same God, just different time. **"I am the Lord and I do not change."** He continues to do mighty signs and wonders in our lives personally. We talk about it in testimony time and maybe even give glory to God with our lips but there is still evidence in our lives we haven't connected to God in the greater way. There is talk about being "sold out" to the Lord and the life simply doesn't match the claim. We are being watched and judged for it by all and justifiably so.

One person is often used as an illustration by the Lord as an example of what to do, who to be and what not to do. Through the scriptures this principle is also punctuated, pointing out what can happen if sin and disobedience pervades a whole society. Persistence in following Jesus wherever He goes brings joy, peace, love and all the other qualities he promises through such a commitment. This is a track that can start with one person and become the dominant factor in an entire nation. As mentioned earlier there were some people in Egypt that were affected by the mighty signs and wonders in Egypt. They were 'god conscious' but did not glorify the Lord in the way the Israelites should have. The Lord provided means to accomplish anything they wanted to, whether it was good or evil, and they did not choose the good very often. The people of God however became more accountable as the miracles continued as well as the 'murmuring and complaining.' Ways other than the Lord's were sought out and implemented when the Lord chose to withhold blessing at any given time. The famed golden calf and evil practices were a response to doubt and unbelief that God would be faithful in what He said. Prior evidence of His faithfulness no longer was honored. This brings us to present day America. It is obvious to even the most vile person that America has been blessed. She has in turn, shared many of the blessings with other nations. What has this bountifulness done? What has any of the Lord's withholding accomplished? We haven't experienced much of the latter. The reason being is found in the bible many times over. Our creativity and skills at finding ways that are not of the Lord to accomplish answers to his approaches to us in whatever capacity He does are sought. (Study and number the shortcuts we have taken for convenience and money.) Based on the cornucopia we have lived in for over 200 years we should be glorifying the God of heaven and earth. His provisions were always meant to be a stamp or vehicle to either thank Him for respite from the 'provisions withheld' and/or to share with others who are in need. The supreme goal of the Lord in all this is to truly allow the relationship between us and Him to develop further by continuous thankfulness, thus acquiring his character. The relationship simply gets better. We grow and mature in Him. As a society that hasn't happened. What did happen? Where did we go wrong to come where we are? How can we set things right?

The old story principle of the frog in the pot of water is found in the bible. Unlike the frog, human beings have been given, by our creator, choices in the matter before we end up in 'hot water'. It is our heart condition that matters. We don't just wake up one day and find ourselves in trouble.

"God is able to bring enough trouble into our lives without our help." RWK

In His realm it is possible to wake up one day to find ourselves in trouble. It happens every day, especially in our physical health. *Ephesians 4:17-19* reads;

"So I tell you this, and insist on it in the Lord, that you must no longer live as the Gentiles do, in the futility of their thinking. They are darkened in their understanding and separated from the life of God because of the ignorance that is in them due to the hardening of their hearts. Having lost all sensitivity they have given themselves over to sensuality so as to indulge in every kind of impurity, with a continual lust for more." NIV

Hardening of a heart requires time and commitment just like softening of the heart. Even Saul's conversion took time if you can see it. God has designed us so that he has potential access to us when we cry out to Him…for Him. That is His best. He does not want me to put off his approaches to me, ignore the conviction by his spirit, and reject the gift of repentance. Ignoring these things results in a very bad life and can continue on to apostasy (abandoning the faith) and ultimately a state of being reprobate—Gr. 96 'adokimos' meaning unapproved or worthless, castaway, rejected. Paul sternly warns of this in Romans 1:28 NIV;

"Furthermore, since they did not think it worthwhile to retain the knowledge of God, he gave them over to a depraved mind, to do what ought not to be done."

They had some of the knowledge of God and chose to waste it up. The desire for the things of this world had become more important than the things of God. The heart began to crave more and more and the mind said yes every time. Remembering the squandered opportunities we had to make the change God was after is a frightening prospect. (Grace)

There once was a woman in an intensive care unit of a hospital. She had severe asthma and its effects were hastened by the woman smoking cigarettes for many years. She had only days to live. I heard her say in tears how sorry she was that she had ignored the obvious convictions that it was the wrong thing to do and now she was paying for it with her life.

With or without the examples of other people's mistakes the Lord has chosen ways tailored to fit each person to let us know where he or she needs to come to. In Christianity the awareness of God becomes heightened and the accountability increases. His provisions are good enough for all of us. When Paul asked the Lord to remove the thorn in the flesh, the Lord's response was, *"My grace is sufficient for thee."* The apostle lived in the light of the Lord's revelation to him personally. His appeal was personal. The Lord's 'no' is a provision. It is his word and his words have life. It can be easy to ignore the Lord only if the heart is bent to do so. Finding myself in a rejected state again can come only by way of choosing moment by moment over time to reject the one who will reject me if I allow it by my own choices. Whatever choices I do make, the Lord will make sure I am provided for. Hopefully I will make the right ones. Somewhere along the line Satan made the initial choice to reject what the Lord had for him. Then he continued on to be lost and rejected forever. He has become an instrument in the hand of God to do whatever it is the Lord wants. Because he now is in the state he finds himself, his ministry has changed. What was once gloriously hailed by the host of heaven as the leader of all the angels was now brought low by the failing to deal with his heart. We may not understand all of the relationship God has with his angels but this issue of heart keeps popping up and it does include these beings as well.

Satan has a unique ministry now. Being this tool in the hand of God, in this way, must be very strange. He knows his time is short, he will end up in the lake of fire and still God uses him to accomplish things on earth and in man. Our usefulness to others is not to be a measuring stick of our relationship with God. How we may be used can indicate much, but our coming to him when he says; "Come unto me" is most important. My relationship with Him will dictate my relationship to him. Satan's relationship with him dictates what his relationship to Him is, hence the manner or capacity God will use him. To us Christians, God's provisions to us may include Satan and or his followers, be it other angels or people. How the Lord comes to us is important. What is most helpful is the examples of Jesus life that the Father will bring us to in our time of need. His provision is constantly flowing. 'Plunge in today and be made complete'. Never stop this and the threat of being in hot water will not be a part of your life.

THE FUNCTION OF GRIEF AND SORROW

God's provisions during our brief stay in this world may include pain and suffering. It has become the Christian's mainstay to immediately start praying for a healing when such actions are initiated by the Lord. Previously mentioned was the fact of two kinds of trouble. The trouble I cause myself and then the trouble the Lord brings into my life. In the deepest sense both are allowed by God but the former is through disobedience and sin while the latter comes directly by the Lord's sovereignty. He not only allows it but may initiate it. In *Job 2:10b* KJV when Job said,

"What? shall we receive good at the hand of God, and shall we not receive evil?"

And in Ecclesiastes 7:14 NIV, Solomon also advances this truth.

"When times are good, be happy; but when times are bad, consider; God has made one as well as the other."

...he (Job) voiced the truth that God does do these things. Why? Among many other reasons there is the addressing the state of the person. A Christian can be the recipient of the Lord's troubles because he is trusting in Him, not trusting in him, or having a sin problem in an area the Lord is trying to clean up. In can be a faith issue and God may want to move the quality of faith up a notch or two. When there are no answers to as why God is doing such a thing, in our agony is the underlying provision of faith to sustain us in that very hour. I can suffer greatly and at the same time have a faith in Him that through His sovereignty he can do what he wants. I realize this and am immediately sustained in that trial. Making a real decision to follow the Lord may come very often without mentioning it. If the Lord has my heart, he now has access to all of me.

For the Christian there are some elements to the principle of suffering that are most divine and intimate between the child of God and God himself. All the attempts at comfort by others are insufficient. Death of a loved one brings this point home to the heart. I can talk to friends, pastors, and even the Lord himself and still the pain remains. In scripture there is nothing found wrong with the existence of this type of pain in a person's life. We may discover some things about God or ourselves during this affliction. In an odd command of the Lord in *Ezekiel 24:15-18*, the Lord spake to the prophet.

"The word of the Lord came to me: "So of man, with one blow I am going about to take away from you the delight of your eyes. Yet do not lament or weep or shed any tears. Groan quietly; do not mourn for the dead. Keep your turban fastened and your sandals on your feet; do not cover the lower part of your face or eat the customary food of mourners. So I spoke to the people in the morning, and in the evening my wife died. The next morning I did as I had been commanded." NIV

Some of the intentions of God during Ezekiel's time of suffering included the approach by God to the state of someone else, namely the house of Israel around Ezekiel. They were not in a good state and needed correction. In our life that may be one of many reasons for the Lord's actions. Whatever is spoken to us may contain within that word the faith and timely strength to carry it out. This is the complete package by God. It is always delivered at the right time, sometimes at the eleventh hour, but always at the right time.

Being counted worthy to suffer at the righteousness of God in me is counted for much in the scriptures. It is in the eyes of God, of great value to qualify for the suffering that comes from Him. In speaking to the Thessalonian church Paul says in 2*Thess. 1:3-5*

"We ought always to thank God for you, brothers, and rightly so, because your faith is growing more and more, and the love every one of you has for each other is increasing. Therefore, among God's churches we boast about your perseverance and faith in all the persecutions and trials you are enduring. All this is evidence that God's judgment is right, and as a result you will be **counted worthy** *of the kingdom of God, for which you are* **suffering**.*" NIV*

We need to understand our position with God before an understanding of what he may be after. Our own state of relationship with Him can tell about the nature of his hurt toward us. One of the most common frets among Christians who are suffering is the lack of understanding. Remember, it may not be wrong to not understand something. However, it is wrong not to understand, when our relationship with God is not where it should be, and that particular understanding should be there as well. This bad relationship produces a lack of understanding. **You can lack understanding during a**

right relationship with God but most often there will be no fretting about it. The heart is in such a condition that it was able to receive the entire revelation from Him and live.

The world and too much of Christianity suffers needlessly from a wrong relationship with the creator thus producing the fret. Fear, lack of faith, doubt, will produce many other ailments not meant for us at all. These things are all God's plan B. They should not be necessary. Jesus said not to worry. He speaks in *Matthew 6:25* by first saying,

"Therefore I tell you, do not worry about your life, what you will eat or drink; or about your body, what you will wear. NIV

He concludes the chapter and subject in the famed verse *33;*

"Therefore do not worry about tomorrow, for tomorrow will worry about itself. Each day has enough trouble of its own."

While God's divine work may be acknowledged in many ways, the issue of his sovereignty trips up many people. Jesus says just prior to these verses in *Matthew 6:24*

"No one can serve two masters. Either he will hate the one and love the other, or he will be devoted to the one and despise the other. You cannot serve both God and money." NIV

There is a preparation being set in place in this verse. God divinely and in his sovereignty is going to have much to do with this subject. He causes what he commands us not to. When we have done all we can do in some particular, (in this case, serving God or money) there may be trouble, causing us to need help for something we may not have caused. Jesus went to the cross through a horrifying path. He caused none of it but obeyed the Father unto death. When we are good stewards of anything God has put into our hands the Lord can still take it away. It may not be punishment. It may not be to "teach us another lesson". It may be for us to count it all joy or to ramp up our faith to another level set by him. Whatever the case is, he says to serve him and not another. That has been the desire of God from the start. **Worrying is not a provision of God**. He **IS** the provision in much and in lack. He should be able to come down and do what he likes without any manifestation of evil on our part. That takes time and work jointly.

Paul gives us solemn warning about allowing ourselves to stay in a condition that God disapproves of in 1 Corinthians 10 in reference to Israel failing to view God's blessings of abundance in the right way. It cost many their lives. Over and over again there was a giving by the Lord God and a taking away by the Lord and still many people failed to break of their lustful spirit. Verses 1 thru 13 states;

"For I do not want you to be ignorant of the fact, brothers, that our forefathers were all under the cloud and that they all passed through the sea. they were all baptized into Moses in the cloud and in the sea. They all ate the same spiritual food and drank the same spiritual drink; for they drank from the spiritual rock that accompanied them, and that rock was Christ. Nevertheless, God was not pleased with most of them; their bodies were scattered over the desert. Now these things

*occurred as examples to keep us from setting our hearts on evil things as they did. Do not be idolaters, as some of them were; as it is written: The people sat down to eat and drink and got up to indulge in pagan revelry. We should not commit sexual immorality, as some of them did—and in one day twenty-three thousand of them died. We should not test the Lord, as some of them did—and were killed by snakes. And do not grumble, as some of them did—and were killed by the destroying angel. These things happened to them as examples and were written down as warnings for us, on whom the fulfillment of the ages has come. So, if you think you are standing firm, be careful that you don't fall! No temptation has seized you except what is common to man. And God is faithful; he will not let you be tempted beyond what you can bear. But when you are tempted, he will **also** provide a way out so that you can stand up under it."* NIV

The key word here is 'also'. This is the indicator that God had something to do with the temptation. This word here is *peirazo* gr. 3985 meaning to 'test'. There are many descriptive terms in the meaning but the point is that there is a testing going on in my life and I get to choose where I am going to get my provision, the provision being offered by God for that time of trial or the provision being offered by Satan through his host of servants. Whatever the choice that I make is, my life will display the results of that choice. God pours life into me and I become an overcomer in Him. Or I will experience death being poured into me having chosen provision from anyone or anything else other than God. Although it may require some difficult decision making, there is nothing too hard for God when he has been considered in such a place. Life or death, I choose. There is no third choice. May we choose God in all things. The alternatives are always there and they are meant to be, otherwise we have a purposeless existence. God tests us. He may use Satan himself to do it but in the Lord there is our hope. Very often we live as if there is only the world's way and not God's. This point is demonstrated by how we live our lives. Doubt, fear, worry and murmuring saturate the church. People in high governmental positions are assailed by Christians who do not yet have the true godly qualities. We are not supposed to make the man or woman in office our savior from the world's woes and we cannot raise our children with qualities we do not yet have ourselves. We will be just creating another person like us while kicking against God by coming against the ones he sends our way to provoke us to himself. We are buying the lie that somehow someone who thinks like us is going to straighten things out. It never stops. The same problems continue to get worse no matter who is in office. May we repent of this doubt and unbelief and come back to the Lord who has made **'the way'** for us. In the following segment, provision from God takes on the depths of our heart.

DESPAIR AND COMFORT

Comfort is a provision by the lord meant to give hope and strong sense of security during a season of what may seem hopeless. The need for comfort should be found in the hands of God and not sought from elsewhere. (I was once comforted by a fruit fly sent from Him.) Unless God reveals differently, our attempt to find comfort in an answer to a question will end in further despair. Why me? Why did it happen to such a nice person? She was so young…and so forth. A Christian's walk with God should be to find comfort in God himself and what he imparts to us in that hour of need. A spiritually blinded person will sulk and grieve at the feet of despair only wanting answers, not the God of the answers. That naturally goes for unbelievers but us Christians as well. We reap what we sow too. Death has a way of bringing out what lies deepest in the survivor(s).

Probably the most famous reference in scripture used with the intention of finding God's comfort for one's self or others is found in the Old Testament, *Psalms 23*. In *verse four part b* we read;

*"your **rod** and your **staff**, they comfort me."* NIV

The word rod here is 'shabet' 7626 Hebrew, meaning 'a stick for punishing, writing, fighting, ruling, walking, etc. Staff in this scripture is 'misheneth' 4938 Hebrew, meaning sustenance or walking stick. The beginning of this verse though says;

'Even though I walk through the valley of the shadow of death, I will fear no evil, for you are with me...'

The Lord has created a circumstance in David's life that requires an acknowledgment of completeness in the Lord. He brings the complete trial of our faith and subsequent faith and trust offered by him in that particular circumstance. If I fail to do my part, despair deepens. Wanting to know why, above trusting Him when I don't know, makes things worse in me and maybe in the situation I find myself in. The decisions I make in my quest to satisfy my own longings can hurt myself and others. This unfortunate principle is the premise for too many relationships between people, including marriage. This false balming affect can bring some type of temporary comfort but actually produces long term dependency on something other than God himself. We see this principle operating everywhere. His desire is for us to receive the trust and faith he is offering at the time of despair, not for us to seek comfort in something he has created.

The rod and staff in this psalm are a means of provision when things get tough. The characteristics of both are much the same in each of these applications. A means of support or sustenance are offered at the time of the trial and David tells us of the comfort in them. *Psalm 23* starts out with

"The Lord is my shepherd". NIV

That is the key to not just this psalm but the whole bible and our walk with the Lord. If the Lord is allowed to be the one guiding me into green pastures and beside the still waters, then with this same relationship intact he will be able to bring me into the valley of the shadow of death and into the presence of my enemies without me running for comfort in something other than him. He may choose to meet me there or deliver me in the eleventh hour but it doesn't matter. He is God and this sovereignty should be acknowledged. Doubting causes much trouble. Moving without him is doubt and that is the flip side of faith.

"Whatever is not of faith is sin." Romans 14:23b KJV

During and after we have been through a trial of our faith there is the ministry of the Holy Spirit to other people. They may watch us suffer and get something during that time but the finished work by God will be used by him to help those in need. My experience now becomes a fashioned work wielded by him to work out the salvation in their lives. *II Corinthians 1:3-7* tells us of this hope.

"Praise be to the God and father of our Lord Jesus Christ, the Father of compassion and the God of all comfort, who comforts us in all our troubles, so that we can comfort those in any trouble with the comfort we ourselves have received from God. For just as the sufferings of Christ flow over into our lives, so also through Christ our comfort overflows. If we are distressed, it is for your comfort and salvation; if we are comforted, it is for your comfort, which produces in you patient endurance of the same sufferings we suffer. And our hope for you is firm, because we know that just as you share in our sufferings, so also you share in our comfort." NIV

I have heard that I cannot give something that I do not have. A right relationship with the Lord makes available to me his **approach at any time**, unhindered by sin, disobedience, or some other end of my own in mind. By his mercy and grace he may still approach me in any state I find myself, but others will suffer at my stalling to get right with God. His best requires a fully devoted heart to him alone, and then his best to others will flow through me to them as well. I am a willing vessel for the Lord to pass through to those he chooses to minister to. He does not want me to choose an alternative to him and he also does not want to choose an alternative for me. If he gets left out, that spells trouble, unnecessary trouble. We may fight against the Lord. This can result, because of who the Lord is, what he does and how he does it. In effect, lip service to say he is Lord may keep the fight going. He remains steadfast and true to his word. He does not waver in what he says. When I begin to understand that, I can begin to acquire things of substance from him in the form of humility, repentance, and good works, I realize these things are a gift of God as *Philippians 2:13* says;

*"for it is God who **works in you** to will and to act according to his good purpose."* (my emphasis) NIV

Provision from God may be hidden, darkened, or obvious and very bright. This may depend upon my heart condition. My investment of time with God will produce the type of susceptibility that is acceptable to him. My response to the Lord's approach in his many ways is dictated by who I am, not Him. This is perhaps one of the greatest acts of love from him to us. While never forcing us to see things his way, our way may be contrasted by his Godly approach. He is the light and we dwell in the dark with the presence of sin. When the contrast of light comes, what happens? We either rejoice because our hearts desire Him or we may become sorrowful or a host of other bad qualities because our hearts reject Him. This was observed where both of these heart conditions existed in one place in Egypt. *In Exodus 11:3 NIV*

"The Lord made the Egyptians favorably disposed toward the people, and Moses himself was highly regarded in Egypt by Pharoah's officials and by the people."

Because we know so well the stories of the plagues of Egypt and subsequent crossing of the Red Sea miraculously, it can be very easy to assume that all the Egyptians fall into the same thinking as their leader. They did not. It is in itself a subtle evidence of the existence of the true and living God. The same thing is happening today. People in power are making decisions based on what they personally want...not their constituents. Some admit it openly. This again is God. The system is coming full circle and it will crumble. Those who are favorably deposed to God (Christians) and those (unbelievers with softening hearts) that are favorably deposed toward his people are being divided from the world's ways of trying to gain in vain. God is everywhere and when we don't believe it...He is nowhere. We will attempt again to solve our problems our way.

When I became a Christian my fervor was like a wild horse. I campaigned against ungodliness in our society. I even wrote notes and accompanying scriptures and put them in cases of beer in the grocery store. I didn't want people to go down the same path I had been. My unbridled zeal was driven by the lack of connection with the Lord. I was operating with my own understanding, not yet knowing the Lord as I ought. When those changes began to occur, I started to settle down. My approach to people began to change as I changed my approach to God's approach to me. I began to realize that though I wanted to do good, the Lord had to be in control with that as well. My suffering for doing something wrong, thinking I was doing good was hailed by me and many others who thought the same way. **We were all deluded**. Many people who had been Christians for years were and still are deluded about this. When God grips the heart and begins to make those changes, the ministry takes on a whole new course. Peter the Apostle went through this personally. This is why he was able to speak about it in—

1 Peter 3: 13-17. "Who is going to harm you if you are eager to do good? But even if you suffer for what is right, you are blessed. Do not fear what they fear; do not be frightened. But in your hearts always set apart Christ as Lord. Always be prepared to give an answer to everyone who asks you to give the reason for the hope that you have (The KJV says: "the hope that lies within you") But do this with gentleness and respect, keeping a clear conscience, so that those who speak maliciously against your good behavior in Christ may be ashamed of their slander. It is better, if it is God's will, to suffer for doing good than for doing evil." NIV

Peter is speaking about **doing** something after we **become** something, not before. Doing good in Him is not the same as my own interpretation of doing good. Peter is not talking about my brand of good. Discernment in the Lord, wisdom in the Lord, all of it must be an outflowing of him, not an outflowing of ourselves with our stamping 'God's will' on it. Like Peter, we can have God illuminate our own experiences that will now become nourishment for others. When that happens, we can now realize that His provisions are not something to be rejected but accepted, to build up our relationship with Him. Though some of his provisions are difficult to accept, he imparts grace to accept them. That connection can 'keep' you, even on the cross.

The most profound act of faith in a child of God may be the act of belief. Belief in truth can come only and obviously because it is true and pure, and those are the very things I am to think about. All this comes down from heaven. *Philippians 4:8 says;*

"Finally, brothers, whatever is true noble, whatever is right, whatever is pure, whatever is lovely, whatever is admirable— if anything is excellent or praiseworthy—think about such things." NIV

My heart condition again comes into play here. It depends on what I am really after. My motives are to be pure. What will happen if they are not pure will open the door to deception of even the finest tuning.

Within the past year for the first time at age 56 I had both my eyes and my ears examined extensively. I had over time lost a tiny fraction of each for different reasons. My ears needed cleaning very much but the noise of the world has taken its toll anyway. Jackhammers, heavy equipment and loud music back in the seventies seemed to be the primary culprit. Under the watchful eyes of a trained audiologist he would go through a wide range of sounds and ask me to respond when I heard them. I seemed to be happy as I often signaled each time I heard the projected sound. He reduced the volume and the tone to complete the test until he compiled a true representation of the status of my hearing. I failed to recognize a couple of very faint low tones. I don't require hearing aids yet but I learned that trying so hard to hear something, sometimes I imagined it. There was nothing there.

My eye test went through the same type of drills. The distance of the objects determined the quality of my sight. I need corrective reading glasses. I didn't see things that weren't there but I was tempted to say yes when something wasn't there. I wanted to pass very much so. That was what was in my heart. It was wrong.

To be at rest in the Lord means my spiritual ears and eyes will be poised to hear and see Him, unhindered by impure motive. The small still voice of is not always meant to be a test, but because of where I am or where I am not, this will determine the keenness of those senses. I can be sure that if I am after something other than God himself that the door has been swung wide open to be lead astray by other voices and other sights. I will come to depend on those things that might have been originally meant to be blessings but now are curses. We change, the Lord does not.

"Don't be deceived, my dear brothers. Every good and perfect gift is from above, coming down from the Father of heavenly lights, who does not change like shifting shadows." James 1:16-17 NIV

It is not a good thing for God to see his children make what he intended for us see and hear, as something else. We even make our sufferings a god. Nothing seems barred from elevating above the one who made it. Our heart is responsible for bringing up or bringing down all of the circumstances in our lives…all of them. If I am humbled there is a reason for it. If I am exalted there is a reason for it. Whatever the case may be there is a provision from the Lord that will accompany that blessing. *James 1:9-10* reads;

"The brother in humble circumstances ought to take pride in his high position. But the one who is rich should take pride in his low position, because he will pass away like a wild flower." NIV

A brother who is humbled and at the same time acknowledges he is in a high position has the correct heart before God. It may be during a time of obedience to the Lord or it may be during time of sinfulness. **Saul** was approached and humbled on the road to Damascus. He was an unbeliever at the time but his mind was transformed immediately when he was struck blind. His heart was changed to serve the Lord, finally His way. **Saul** had been a staunch enemy of Christianity and his reputation followed him wherever he went and at the time, he in the NIV,

"was still breathing out murderous threats against the Lord's disciples." Acts 9:1

Jesus was humbled in many ways yet he did not sin. There were times when he could have disobeyed his Father and went his own way during this time of trial but he did not. After he told the disciples about the suffering they were going to endure, he gave them a command in,

Luke 21:14 "But make up your mind not to worry beforehand how you will defend yourselves." NIV

The Lord himself was tested in the ways common to man. When he was betrayed in the garden of **Gethsemane** (oil press—1068Greek) he made it known what he could have done but did not. Twelve legions of angels were at his disposal to take care of the problems of the moment. Jesus learned obedience through the things he suffered and became obedient until death, even the death of the cross. **He had determined**

beforehand what he was telling the disciples to do. (My emphasis)

We as Christians disobey. While the potential is always there we do not have to disobey. There is nothing good to be gained by disobedience. I do not have to defend myself. I do not have to complain about the price of gasoline or what the President is doing. The quality of relationship between the children of the Lord and himself is such that these elementary things should not have to be mentioned. We should have moved on to greater things in Him but the current state of the (majority) church is exceedingly repulsive. May we determine to repent and go on with God "Withersoever he goest" when he calls. After that, the next step is "doing".

"Suffering should not ever become a god." RWK

WORKS

In the quest to become "tight" with God it would be right to say that although the intention is good, it is only a door to the perfect work. Responding correctly, **now,** to the Lord compiles a track record of acceptance by Him. Because of the state of all humanity, the discipline of fearing God and shunning evil can only come from Him. On our early path in the Lord we may make decisions that seem to come from us and they do **seem** to work…for a season. (Some are correct) God always wants to break in at a certain point and take over our lives completely, preferable from the start. This will depend on the condition I as an individual can be found. When the time came, Saul got it immediately, but it took a while for Peter. We can see all through scripture the times and reasons why the Lord was able or not, to break in and take over a person's life. This captivation by God is the precursor to a life of 'works' in the Christian.

Shortly after I got saved I had this idea that I was going to be an evangelist. Back in the early and mid eighties I watched what I thought were all the powerhouses of evangelism on the television. I hung the direction in my life on every word they spoke. What I really needed was to understand that the time had come to go to God myself and participate in the plan He had for me and I had to admit I did not know what that was. All I knew was after listening to everyone else for a season, there was more than that. There is that intimate, one to one love for the Lord and His love for me. I intended to let all else go and finally seek the Lord for myself.

After a time of that aspect in one's life, the issue of works will then come into play. My heart condition will always show God what he can do with me. He has to tailor His ministry to me based on that. It is possible with God to bring into my life the heart of humility and acts of boldness at the same time. *1Samuel 17 12-15* tells us this proof.

*"Now David was the son of an Ephrathite named Jesse, who was from Bethlehem in Judah. Jesse had eight sons, and in Saul's time he was old and well advanced in years. Jesse's three oldest son's had followed Saul to the war: The firstborn was Eliab; the second, Abinidab; and the third, Shammah. David was the youngest. The three oldest followed Saul but David went **back and forth** from Saul to tend his father's sheep at Bethlehem."* NIV

David had done something that his brothers did not. We can see the manifestation of God's work done previously in him come out in the form of tending his brothers in battle and then going back home to tend sheep. The most profound exhibit of David's relationship up to that point with God (at least in scripture) is found several verses later when Saul tried to disqualify David from being able to approach Goliath, and David's subsequent defense of God's reputation through him. *1Samuel 17:34-37* says:

But David said to Saul, "Your servant has been keeping his father's sheep. When a lion or a bear came and carried off a sheep from the flock, I went after it, struck it and rescued the sheep from its mouth. When it turned on me, I seized it by its hair, struck it and killed it. Your servant has killed both the lion and the bear; this uncircumcised Philistine will be like one of them, because he has defied the armies of the living God. The Lord who delivered me from the paw of the lion and the paw of the bear will deliver me from the hand of this Philistine." NIV

David was being put by the Lord into a new aspect of ministry. He was being brought out away from his home (where the initial greater work was done) and into a great contrasting aspect, meeting, with the faith God had worked in, against an enemy who was viewed by everyone else, as too mighty and strong. The work done in a person is revealed by the teacher and master who brings an antagonist into that person's life. It may be, as it is in this case, another person. It may be an event great or small. Whether it be a personal affliction or another tool in the hand of God to bring out who we are, or aren't, it will happen. David was exercising what he possessed. It is evident by his words prior to killing Goliath that this was the case. When he proclaimed what he had done to the bear and the lion, he trusted God would also do the same for him in battle. The real work was done in private relationship with God and the Lord moved the battle from the closet into the street for all to see. David passed that test. His life had taken a new turn which would **eventually reveal everything in him.**

"If I act on only my belief of God's character, I may right be about Him but wrong in the direction. Knowledge of his character does not necessarily mean imparted direction for me. This is the big trip up that causes contention and division in the church."

Even the world with its original installment of God in them can discern correctly some of the do's and don'ts, they just do not always attribute the source of that direction to anyone else other than themselves. That creates the sense of being a god when the real God is not acknowledged. When works are done, the heart behind the work is of utmost importance and does come first. *2 Corinthians 9:7* echoes the point.

"Each man should give what he has decided in his heart to give, not reluctantly or under compulsion, for God loves a cheerful giver." NIV

It is important to say that giving the heart to the Lord on a daily basis will keep much of everything that comes against that effort, out of the way, maybe even all of it. We can be deceived into thinking God approves when there is something we should have done and we have not.

Running rampant in the church is the lie that "God wants to bless you with things or money," while at the same time there are things that have not been done and should have. In *Proverbs 28:13* we see perhaps the greatest example of this.

"He who conceals his sins does not prosper but whoever confesses and renounces them finds mercy." NIV

In these last days the word, prosper, is brought into the church and is too often referred to in the fiscal sense. In this scripture, 'prosper' means "to push forward, go over, be meet, be profitable." Hebrew 6743 tsaleach. A life is stalled while this wrong condition is met. Reluctance to confess and renounce or forsake sin keeps a person from going forward in the kingdom of God. We see people prosper all the time financially and still have sin not dealt with. The key to all of it is the fear of the Lord. In the very next verse we see why God drives home the point of taking care of the sin problem.

Proverb 28:14 "Blessed is the man who always fears the Lord, but he who hardens his heart falls into trouble." NIV

In the previous scripture we find mercy not money. In the last verse we find trouble and that may include money. Money may be a blessing or a curse. Again, my heart condition makes it one or the other but not both (to me).

In the initial stages of our works we are going to experience the need of a measure of patience from God that will sustain us in the hour of need. If we do not fear God any longer or fall into a misunderstanding we may allow an array of substitutes into our lives. The pressure is on, deadlines have to met and time is running out. Oh, the fear of loss and I drive to rescue myself in the heat of the moment! Which way am I going to go, God or some other way? What happened to Jesus when faced with this? *In Matthew 4:4* his answer covers every other problem he faced as well as ours.

"But He answered and said, "It is written, Man shall not live by bread alone but by every word that proceedeth out of the mouth of God." KJV

It doesn't matter what the temptation is, or from, when it comes, or even why, this point carries with it the resolution to everything. In the other examples where Satan tested Jesus, our Lord demonstrated this truth. He was living by every word from the Father, not an evil intentioned quote from the devil. His works were birthed out of drawing on God the Father with a pure heart, sinlessness, and obedience. Any or all of these qualities did not excuse him from being tried and tested but rather only proved for us that we now have the same access to the Father and can get the same results, that being mercy, not millions of dollars.

"REST CAN BE TO WORK WHAT SILENCE CAN BE TO COMMUNICATION." RWK

Rest in the Lord is so much different than neglect of duty. This principle began with Him. *Genesis 2:2-3* says:

"By the seventh day God had finished the work he had been doing; so on the seventh day he rested from all his work. And God blessed the seventh day and made it holy, because on it he rested from all the work of creating that he had done." NIV

While there may be many other reasons why he did that, we will work with what we have been given. The Sabbath Day has been established and instituted into the schedule of humanity.

Resting in the Lord is accompanied by his perfect peace, humility, the fear of God, and maybe other aspects depending on the circumstances. A child of God who is captivated enough by the Lord in this area has begun to take notice more readily when it is time to rest or work. Other people can take notice when you are obedient because of some of the occasions of work or rest in your life. This begins in the prayer closet. In early stages it is with good intention I may think it is time to pray, read the bible or some other good habit I have that fosters my relationship with God. He may break in and start a new work, prompting me to take notice that there is more to learn about work and rest. I have gotten flustered because He sent an interruption more than once to get my attention. It was time to stop or not even start reading or praying. After blaming the devil a few times for the phone or the doorbell, etc. I got the point. A peace that I never had began to enter the life. *Luke 10:40-42* NIV illustrates this.

"But Martha was distracted by all the preparations that had to be made. She came to him and asked, "Lord, don't you care that my sister has left me to do the work by myself? Tell her to help me!" "Martha, Martha," the Lord answered, "You are worried and upset about many things, but only one thing is needed. Mary has chosen what is better, and it will not be taken away from her."

Martha's understanding of the order of things was not the same as the Lord's and he had to tell her when she became frustrated as a result of her own understanding. (Even writing about "rest" first and then "works" hasn't made much sense to me but this is the order it is supposed to be. Like Martha, my own understanding is not to be leaned on either.)

Rest is something the Lord gives us.

Joshua 1:13 "Remember the command that Moses the servant of the Lord gave you: The Lord your God is giving you rest and has granted you this land."

Jesus openly says this truth in *Matthew 11:28-30.*

"Come unto me, all you who are weary and burdened, and I will give you rest. Take my yoke upon you and learn from me, for I am gentle and humble in heart, and you will find rest for your souls. For my yoke is easy and my burden is light." NIV

We can easily associate 'rest' with the physical and not give much thought about what Jesus is saying here. He was gentle, humble of heart because he was yoked with the Father. There is the living out of the characteristics of the one we yoke ourselves to. We become just like whatever we submit ourselves to. If it is something else other than God then whatever characteristics that thing has will begin to show in my life. There may a conscious effort to suppress or hide it but in short or long it will come out in my words or actions. We see this in operation with people who have seemed to get away with it for a season but the Lord came down and exposed those things. In politics, business, and religion, the secrets hidden from man for a while reacted to the power of God coming in a greater way in these last days. Then, out it comes. Many are shocked that a person with great reputation and influence was really doing this all the time and we didn't know. It is a work of God and it is best for the person to get things straight. Many people express the feeling of relief now that they don't have to run any more.

What are the consequences of not resting when I am supposed to? Well, if I am not resting, that means I am doing something. What am I doing? Whatever it is, I can be sure I have cast God aside and am running under my own power. I can go for a while but am destined to tire in a wrong way. (You can tire in a right way) KJV *Proverbs 22:3* tells us,

"A prudent man foreseeth the evil, and hideth himself: but the simple pass on, and are punished." The NIV puts it this way: *"A prudent man sees danger and takes refuge, but the simple keep going and suffer for it."*

The crux of the message here is not only in reference to willful sin but any deviation from the path we have been on with God. Resting when God wants us to rest is better than staring at the subject and thinking that if I don't act now all will be lost. As a result we reach out in fear when the heat is on. The Father was able to break into Jesus' life and wake him in the boat by those who hadn't yet gotten the messages the Lord was trying to teach them. They had their eyes in other places and it showed by their doubt and fears. Jesus was not frustrated by being wakened, (that would be complaining) but he was chiding the disciples for not having something they should have had by now. They were accountable for that. This is a shadow of the world and unfortunately too many in the church. Although each group has its own set of standards the principle is the same. A prophet can be calm in a storm or be urgent when all is calm. Many will not understand, because the right path in their own life was forsaken.

Rest is a work. It is just as much a work as works when God is in it. Obedience to cease from a God ordained work is as common as the active work itself, thus rest can be a command of the Lord just like a command to work may be. *Psalm 37:7* KJV could not be more obvious.

"Rest in the Lord and wait patiently for him: fret not thyself because of him who prospereth in his way, because of the man who bringeth wicked devices to pass".

Although this is not necessarily a ceasing from the physical work, it clearly is not just a suggestion or recommendation from the one who made us. If the Lord speaks that into my life, I am to rest in the Lord. He imparts his rest to me as I obey. The provision is there for my work. Rest is now my work. There are reasons in this case why I may need this type of rest. *Verses 8-11* tell us.

"Cease from anger, and forsake wrath: fret not thyself in any wise to do evil. For evildoers shall be cut off: but those who wait upon the Lord, they shall inherit the earth".

What will be the result of my obedience to such a command? In *verse 23* the question is answered.

"The steps of a good man are ordered by the Lord: and he delighteth in his way."

When the Lord asks or commands us to give him something there is always his replacement for it; more of himself. Doubt and unbelief are not commands from the Lord but they cause us to try and fix things ourselves. We don't rely on God but choose a way he commands us not to go. The wrong way can be very dangerous and when we are blinded enough even

God may aid us in that direction and our blindness won't see it. *Mark 14:32-41* makes this bold claim as Jesus aids three disciples in our subject. Keep in mind the progression, the Lord tells them each step of the way what they are doing. He does not give up on them, but gives them the liberty of choice.

*"And they came to a place which was named Gethsemane: and he saith to his disciples, Sit ye here, while I shall pray. And he taketh with him Peter, James and John, and began to be sore amazed, and to be very heavy: And he saith unto them, "My soul is exceeding sorrowful unto death: tarry ye here and watch". And he went forward a little, and fell on the ground, and prayed that, if it were possible, the hour might pass from him. And he said, "Abba, Father, all things are possible unto thee; take away this cup from me: nevertheless not what I will, but what thou wilt". And he cometh, and findeth them sleeping, and saith unto Peter, Simon, sleepest thou? "Couldest not thou watch one hour? Watch ye and pray, lest ye enter into temptation. The spirit truly is ready, but the flesh is weak". And again he went away, and prayed, and spake the same words. And when he returned, he found them asleep again, (for their eyes were heavy,) neither wist they what to answer them, **Sleep on now**, **and take your rest**: it is enough, the hour is come; behold, the son of Man is betrayed into the hands of sinners. Rise up, let us go; lo, he that betrayeth me is at hand."* KJV

It was not God's rest Jesus was talking about, it was their rest. We can only assume what the three men would have gotten had they obeyed. Maybe Peter wouldn't have been in a spirit to cut off the servant's ear just a short time later or denying the Lord those three times. What God had in store we just don't know. We do know it would have been good compared to what they got or lost due to disobedience. In the Lord it would not make any difference what it was. Look what Jesus got for obeying the Father. That is why He is our perfect example...always, for richer or poorer, better or worse, in sickness and in health. There is only victory in Him.

Resting in the Lord and entering his rest may or may not be the same thing. Resting in the Lord can be times of acknowledging that you have that quality and some time later you discover you don't, for whatever reason. Entering the Lord's rest is a life that is captivated by God and is entirely surrendered to him. Him having me is different than me having him. I now live, move and have my being in Him. That is his rest. When a person has gone from resting in the Lord to entering the Lord's rest, his or her consistency will produce a hunger and a longing in other people who are initially hungry for God in the first place. The price must be paid for each of us who long for that relationship with the Lord. The price is my **self**. However, even making the relationship itself an 'object of affection' will delay the process because sincerity and motive must be pure.

Times of resting in the Lord along the way, is the precursor to entering the Lord's rest. Each person will know when they have entered the Lord's rest and know they cannot give it to someone else. They wisely handle everything in helping others on their own way. This is the definition of truly 'making disciples'. Living, and proclaiming the word of God is a human being's responsibility and becomes God's best intended means to begin to multiply His kingdom. The seeds are planted and watered and of course He increases it by His spirit.

The Lord's work is manifested in this world in uncountable but accountable ways. His works are still being discovered in the plant and animal kingdom. New species are found every year in remote places. Our view of these things is again a matter of the heart. There are folks who esteem creation above the creator and get into trouble doing so. Being in awe of God's creation must be bridled because it can lead to false beliefs. There are great people who make accurate observations about what God has made but fail to credit the one who made them. When an entire nation falls into this trap, snares are tripped because of the sinful state of the people and the trouble that ensues. In *Romans 1:18-25* Paul accents this fact. (This whole point bears strongly worth repeating)

"The wrath of God is being revealed from heaven against all godlessness and wickedness of men who suppress the truth by their wickedness, since what may be made known about God is plain to them. For since the creation of the world God's invisible qualities—his eternal power and divine nature—have been clearly seen, being understood from what has been made, so that men are **without excuse***. For although they knew God, they neither glorified him as God nor gave thanks to him, but their thinking became futile and their foolish hearts were darkened. Although they claimed to be wise, they became fools and exchanged the glory of the immortal God for images made to look like mortal man and birds and animals and reptiles. Therefore God gave them over to the sinful desires of their hearts to sexual impurity for the degrading of their bodies with one another. They exchanged the truth of God for a lie, and worshipped and served created things rather than the Creator—who is forever praised. Amen."* NIV

Before and after we come to God these things are never the kind of works he wants us to get into. This was all of course, over a period of time, the relentless pursuit of fulfilling the desires of their heart. (Quite a contrast to entering the Lord's rest). Whether we are aware of it or not we all do works as a response to the one who has made us. '**Which works**' now become more important. Referring again to the animal kingdom, many works of God can become clear in their behavior alone and with other creatures. We will see there is much that we previously wouldn't dare assign to God's credit or blame depending what mindset you or I have. The Lord has promised us there are going to be some changes in this area. But there first must be acquired a relationship with God. This is work to be done and then the knowledge will follow.

Isaiah 11:6-9 The wolf will live with the lamb, the leopard will lie down with the goat, the calf and the lion and the yearling together; and a little child will lead them. The cow will feed with the bear, their young will lie down together, and the lion will eat straw like the ox. The infant will play near the hole of the cobra, and the young child put his hand into the viper's nest. They will neither harm or destroy on my holy mountain, for the earth will be full of the knowledge of the Lord as the waters cover the sea. NIV

In the subject of works it is more than essential to learn about discovering what I am to do **in God**. Doing things **for God** is not to be the primary view of the Christian. Being aware that I am doing something for the Lord is not necessarily meaning I am not doing it in him but it also may mean just that. If that is the motivation behind why I do something I can be sure I am operating at a distance. The fact that we can do something out of our own volition and ask God to bless it is not the life or relationship he wants with us. In the beginning it may seem right and noble but this error should be corrected. When there is no unction, leading, anointing, or direction and you get a check against it…just don't do it. If the prevailing force in my life has been doing things for God, hearing this was wrong may leave me with a feeling of being 'out in left field' without the Lord. It is tough to swallow and somewhat frightening. Many years ago I once snuck out of bed early in the morning to go to a pancake house to get my wife's favorite pancakes. She always wanted to be served breakfast in bed and I wanted to surprise her. I went to the pancake house and they wouldn't give me any to go. They said it was illegal. I pleaded to no avail. I returned home to a wife sitting up in bed with the light on, wondering where I had been all night. Well, I obviously did not have the proof I needed to show her where I really was. I begged her to believe my story. It took a long time to accomplish that. Why? Because I was not really the kind of husband I was supposed to be in the first place. This was my work, my own little project. I hadn't established a relationship with her that I could be easily trusted with my answer when I walked in the door with nothing…

…and so it is with God. We should be aware a person doesn't enter the kingdom of God from the world of rebellion a spit polished child of Christ. Sounds infantile but unfortunately it is a place where too many people remain after a long time as a Christian. But now we begin to realize there is or was more to this 'works' thing than we thought. Maybe we couldn't put our finger on the source of stagnation or there has been something troubling us about where we are as a Christian and could not figure out what it is. Life, mercy and love still flow from God to his people. It has not ceased. Works will come out of the relationship, not out of seeing a need, filling it, thus creating a well advertised sense of self satisfaction. If the relationship has been established to His liking then He now has something to work with.

CONTRASTING WORKS.

Jesus shows us in the scriptures the principle of difference between the spiritual and the natural world when it comes to Him personally. Both worlds affected him differently. That is one of the humbling elements about Him. Even though he created everything he still became subject to it having profound affect on the aspect of his humanity.

Daniel 3:24-25 Then King Nebuchadnezzar leaped to his feet in amazement and asked his advisors, "Weren't there three men that we tied up and threw into the fire?" They replied, "Certainly, O king." He said, "Look! I see four men walking around in the fire, unbound and unharmed, and the fourth looks like a son of the gods." NIV

Whether the fourth person in the fire was an angel or Jesus, there is not any indication that this feat was burdensome or stressful. Whoever it was made it clear by their actions that the power of the Father was there and it produced no outward evidence of stress. It appeared like a walk in the park for the fourth person as well as the three children of Israel. This scenario in the bible is contrasted by another story.

Matthew 26:36-38 Then Jesus went with his disciples to a place called Gethsemane, and he said to them, "Sit here while I go over there and pray." He took Peter and the two sons of Zebedee along with him, and he began to be sorrowful and troubled. Then he said to them, "My soul is overwhelmed with sorrows to the point of death. Stay here and keep watch with me." NIV

Luke's version of the account includes;

Luke 22:43-44 An angel from heaven appeared to him and strengthened him. And being in anguish, he prayed more earnestly, and his sweat was like drops of blood falling to the ground. NIV

In the Daniel reference, a spiritual being manifested, and had the purpose of surviving an obvious fire kindled to destroy some people. This person is not mentioned with agony prior to, or during, this work. Jesus in the second illustration clearly experiences agony before he goes to the cross. The nature of each of these works by the Lord is different in many ways but the major point is the adjustment God makes according to what **he** sees as the need. A burden placed on someone will always have the power and sustenance from the Lord according to as he sees fit. That particular adjustment may seem unfair at times. Too much or too little is our cry. The true distinction though, in this case, is that Jesus has to call on the Father for help in resisting the thought of changing his mind about why He came here. It was truly a spiritual battle. That fight manifested itself in our Lord's words as well as his body. The first story was to rescue three people naturally, the second was to rescue the whole human race spiritually. Each job required its own degree of power from God.

Luke 5:21-26 The Pharisees and the teachers of the law began thinking to themselves, "Who is this fellow who speaks blasphemy? Who can forgive sins but God alone?" Jesus knew what they were thinking and asked, "Why are you thinking these things in your heart? Which is easier to say, "Your sins are forgiven, or to say, "Get up and walk'? But that you may know that the Son of Man has authority on earth to forgive sins..." He said to the paralyzed man, "I tell you, get up, take your mat and go home." Immediately he stood up in front of them, took what he had been lying on and went home praising God. NIV

The easier part was healing the man. The easier part was walking in the fire. Jesus may have walked in the fire seemingly with no effort, but the garden and the cross...that was something else. Many stories and sermons have been written and preached about how God will sustain you and I during a trial in our life but the real battle is in the mind and spirit. When corrections are made there with God in the garden, everything else is covered. We can be healed of something physically and never leave our position of rebellion. We can fall back into it as well. The real battle though, must be fought in the presence of the Lord. This is why so few and great miracles are not following those who 'believe' because real belief according to God's definition is lacking. **The works are not joined to God by real belief.** Stories from other lands about miracles happening are easily taken as something we may want to happen here in the United States. What stands between us and those miracles? A desire applied to know God himself in sincerity. The Lord does do miracles in our land but there is obvious evidence he is withholding much because of what we have become. Our land is filled with violence, perversion, injustice, all the things he hates. And it is in great abundance, not just pockets of it. These are works that bring wrath and destruction, not the blessings we think we deserve.

There are things that God expects from me that qualify as a person who is a recipient of certain blessings from him. As I respond to the promptings of the Lord in my own life he is able to build on what I have offered him, essentially **my heart**. God is not fooled or mocked by my insincerity. He has the sovereign right to dispense himself at his choosing. As we look around us we can readily see the alleged disproportionate dispensation of God. To put it bluntly, the Lord acts like he is unfair in his giving and taking. When a relationship with him it cultivated enough corporately, then understanding will alleviate some of this misunderstanding. For example: Just because I can tell you he is always fair and not unjust doesn't mean you will understand it. A price has to be paid for this understanding and God expects no less from anyone (until his appointed time). It sure appears like this is not true at times doesn't it?

Regardless of the state of individuals and all peoples as a whole, God is moving on with his plan. Evidence of His works and evidence of our works are progressing to fulfill the scriptures without delay or altering. Jesus talked about things that were evil, happening to Him as 'fulfilling the scriptures'. Which scriptures am I fulfilling? Am I participating in evil works or good works? Whichever it may be, I can be assured that it all is accumulating a record that will be brought into judgment. It is constantly possible to allow God to judge my every thought, word, or deed as he brings this knowledge to me. That is the acceptable time of the Lord. I must strike when the iron is hot. There may be tears in the night but rejoicing in the morning. Pay the price to get into the relationship rightly with God then it will not matter what state you are in.

I tell you the truth, anyone who has faith in me will do what I have been doing. He will do even greater things than these, because I am going to the father. John 14:12 NIV

Jesus was living a life that meant giving his heart to the father and doing His works. Our Lord had to get this life from a place we cannot see with our naked eye, from a place and person unseen. Everyone who experienced Jesus experienced the Father. Now Jesus had completed his work on this earth in his bodily form and was leaving to go to the place where he got this life. What he was telling the disciples was that they were going to have to do exactly what he had done while they are still here. Go to God the father and now Jesus who is God the Son and get this life He had gotten…if they want to. As we see in scriptures there was evidence that some had chosen to take up their cross and follow Jesus and many more who would not. It was and always will be a choice. God can and may lead me to the water but it is up to me to bend over or kneel down and drink. If God gets his way with me, that is all that should matter because then the good aspect of the scriptures will be fulfilled in my life. And in these last days there will be things done that will be greater than what he did while he was here in bodily form. Start there and the Lord will have something to build on. Do not worry. He has said that he would "Not Leave Us Nor Forsake Us."

Hebrews 13:5 Keep your lives free from the love of money and be content with what you have, because God has said, "Never will I leave you; never will I forsake you." NIV

A SPECIAL SECTION ON RELATIONSHIP

As mentioned before, the element of God putting a measure of himself in each of us during our creation is evidenced by the witness of the spirit. In these last days we find ourselves blinded to many facets of this truth by the way we treat each other.

The Lord gave us the initial installment and it is up to us to come to him for the continuation of that pouring in us more of himself. It is simple. God created man and had a relationship with him. Sin has come into the world and interfered with that relationship but there is a way out. Jesus Christ, the Son, came into this world to give each and every person the opportunity to switch back onto the track to know God by turning from the sinful nature in the heart (repentance) and actively seeking the one who made us for this renewed relationship. Either I respond to his knocking on my heart about that truth or I don't.

What happens to me when I say yes to Jesus' approach with this act of love? My relationship with him changes and my relationship with his other created people changes. By his spirit I am now aligned with his will and can pursue him with all my heart, mind, soul, and strength.

After the initial acts of repentance and commitment to know him better there is an ongoing availability of God to aid and assist me in all things. There are also the drawings and temptations of the still present evils trying to keep me from the improvement efforts on my part to really know my creator better. I get to decide which force gets me. No matter how hard things may seem (or actually are), God our Father, Jesus, and the Holy Spirit are the only ones who can live up to what they say. They will not leave me. They will not forsake me. They are here with me no matter what anyone else says or does. His life now pours into me according to my commitment to know Him.

When my relationship with God increases, so does my relationship with others. How I treat other people will be evidence as to what lengths I went to the Lord in sincerity and over time. When we look around us what do we see? We see this truth operating in the lives of other people too. We get to observe with our eyes, ears, and spirit where others have succeeded or failed in their response to God in all of this. God is not at fault. If I say or do things that are not of God toward others, I obviously need more of God in my life.

I have a relationship with every other person on the face of the earth because of this. The most pronounced example is politics. I may agree or not agree with what a politician says or does. What comes out of my mouth both in content and how I say it will give myself and others an indication of how much I have pursued to know the one who made both of us. I am not supposed to do what God says not to, especially what unbelievers may be doing. In reference to this, Jude reminds us of the stark reality and its consequence.

Jude 9,10 In the very same way, these dreamers pollute their own bodies, reject authority and slander celestial beings. But even archangel Michael, when he was disputing with the devil about the body of Moses, did not dare to bring a slanderous accusation against him, but said, "The Lord rebuke you!" Yet these men speak abusively against whatever they do not understand; and what things they do understand by instinct, like unreasonable animals—these are the very things that destroy them. NIV

There is this pervasive truth occupying many a person in the church. Have nothing to do with it! While it is true that people in power seem to be doing things we do not agree with, we got what we paid for. Since God has been rejected as the ruler over man he is now bringing some things to bear that will not be stopped. If you or I have not been continuing an effort to know God we will be left in the hands of the very ones we proclaim as our enemies(in an unrighteous way). This is not God's will but the results of our own actions to try and rule ourselves. Where has it got us? Repent and come back to the Lord! He awaits a repenting heart. We can have life from heaven even amidst whatever is happening. We don't have to go the *way of Cain, Balaam's error*, or *Korah's rebellion*. (Jude 11)

IN CLOSING

I cannot challenge you to do anything. Unless the Lord is really speaking through me it will be a dead thing. Through my blindness and good intentions over the years, I have helped what I thought were many people in need. If each one of them had been in the Lord I might have gotten a pass because they all would have understood where I was really coming from. (Look at Elihu in Job) Responding to the Lord is really the point.

I am now at a loss for words because I am supposed to be. Many things are being said today but the speaker as well as the hearer, are only helping each other groom something less than God intends for both. May the Lord be allowed to grip our hearts so he gets what he is after. He should be able to do what he wants with us. Job made an observation concerning the Lord's workings in his life at the time.

"Yet if I speak, my pain is not relieved; and if I refrain, it does not go away." Job16:6 NIV

Despite the place Job had found himself he was fit enough in God to realize he actually had not come far enough. There was and is always more to God. Being unable to move by any one of my own faculties and the **acknowledgement of it** is the beginning of something new in the Lord. I'm helpless, in need and destitute without Him.

The response in many to the preaching of the love of God is a continuation of the same practices, habits, and works that may not have originated in the Lord. In the current state of particularly the dwellers in the United States and wherever these practices were exported, the message was supposed to be that of the cross of Christ.

There is a conclusion of a plan of God's currently undergoing an observation by the elect. It is just that conclusion on His part that justifies urgency on ours. Before the Titanic sank, it broke in half but still stayed afloat for a while before it went two and a half miles to the bottom. It is in that exact place we find ourselves. Blindness pervades those who refuse to believe what is obvious. It is the Christian's responsibility to maintain a right relationship with God under any and all circumstances without being influenced to anything different by such circumstances. While it is true that God loves us he has also set in place guidelines and through testings, has made available to us the power to carry them out. Life imparted to us is only a decision away when the Lord brings himself to our attention. Everything about God matters…even his breath. There is life or death in it.

Genesis 2:7 NIV "The Lord God formed the man from the dust of the ground and breathed into his nostrils the breath of life, and the man became a living being"

Isaiah 40:7 NIV "The grass withers and the flowers fall because the breath of the Lord blows on them."

Who is the Lord that we would ascribe such things as we do? Isn't it true that we have forsaken the one who made us and by his great love and patience has given clearly, much time to turn from our wicked ways and return to Him in our helpless state? Jesus Christ came into this world to save us. He also came here for another reason. Even though he knows all, it is still his hope that once we are saved that we would continue to come to him and draw his life, thus making the relationship better than it was before. That has not happened as much as he wants and that is why things other than the cross are being proclaimed. The characteristics of God are only effects and not the cause. When He is made the great cause then his character becomes important.

Whatever price that may be now paid to seek and know God will in effect be overshadowed by Him, thus the sense of personal loss will mean nothing. Amen

The End

****

NOTES TO PONDER AND STUDY

We must always use the standard of God rather than the standard of the world. God is condemned by the world. Is God unfair? Is He unjust? If the standard we are using is the world's, then the answers are yes to both. In reality He is not unfair, He is not unjust. Look around. What do you see? There seems to be much **unfairness** and certainly many cases of **injustice**. The guilty go free and the innocent are condemned. Was Jesus guilty? No. Who do we follow? God speaks in many scriptures about injustice. It originates in the hearts of men. The Lord will treat us as we treat Him and he has everything to use as a tool to accomplish that.

FOR STUDY: What is a person doing when he is resting in the Lord? What aspects are there to note about this type of rest? What is entering the Lord's rest? Benefits etc...

When God shows up, there is always a response. Whether it is a good response or a bad depends on several factors. Whatever the case will be there will never be neutrality about it. Even lukewarmness is a response, be it a bad one. Enemies come together when the Lord makes a mess of something that affects all people in the realm in which they live. Natural disasters bring unity to entire nations who are at odds with each other to supply the needs of the afflicted. After the storm though, we will see a recoiling back to business as usual. Small groups or countries demonstrate this principle back as far as history is recorded. The presence of God through his naturally supernatural events makes peoples' differences mean nothing, but only temporarily. The lack of the knowledge of God and his ways brings out the survival instinct to the greatest degrees when there is calamity or trauma. A person can overcome many things in many ways but he or she can do nothing without the Lord. Does he get the credit or glory? How often he does not.

Within our society there are two primary reasons not to trust a man. One; because you know him and two; because you don't. I will not trust God when I do not know him. There may be an imparted exception. If I really know Him I can have trust that he knows what he is doing. Can I know him and still doubt? Yes. Read the examples in both the Old and New Testaments. Be careful with this topic. There is also a place where implicit trust in God is demonstrated regardless of circumstances in a person's life. There are examples of that in the bible as well.

I have left some of the questions unanswered the closer I got to the end of this manual. There has been a tapering off of some aspects of truth, knowledge, and description of God's character. It is my hope that you, the reader were hungry for God before you read all of this and maybe became aware of some things that aided your desire for more of Him. Searching, meditating, waiting and prayer, bolstering the life you do have, will increase. In the following section there are some questions posed, suggestions made and points alluded to, to help you on your way in God. Prayerfully consider these things while you move on in the Lord. The Lord bless you.

What is **profiling**? WEBSTER: the act or process of extrapolating information about a person based on known traits or tendencies. Extrapolate: to infer from values within an already observed interval. (Look at again) Infer: to derive as a conclusion from facts or premises. While we are most likely familiar with criminal profiling, the principles are the same application. We won't be profiling a criminal or do any racial profiling. The end of the matter is that we will fear God and keep his commandments because we will know him better and realize it is our duty. (see Ecclesiastes 12:13,14)

BASIC PROFILING

1. BOLO—means 'Be On the Lookout'
2. APB—means All Points Bulletin—Both of these aspects can be acquired because of the witness of other people. Things such as clothes, vehicles, maybe even a tattoo or the direction they were heading, may be limited in scope but will aid in the search for the person(s). It could be a lost person as well. It is important to note that the more witnesses there are does not necessarily mean accuracy is greater. It may in effect be the opposite. Many people see and hear things differently. Auto accidents are a good example.

PSYCHOLOGICAL PROFILE

This aspect is used in absence of or a supplement to physical evidence. There may be notes left, as well as the state of the scene where the person was last observed by eyewitnesses or by evidence they were there. What kind of food, drink, and many other pieces of evidence may reveal what kind of person(s) we are dealing with.

It may be easy to profile someone we know well but these profiling helps are meant to discover and predict the person's next move of whom is currently not known to the person who is doing the searching.

PREDICTIVE PROFILING

This would be guessing which people are likely to commit an act that hasn't happened yet. There may be 'cumulative similarities' that indicate a particular group or program in which our subject might have originated from. Maybe a religious or political motivation is the driving force behind an act.

The **experience** of the 'profiler' comes into play. That does not always guarantee success but it weighs heavily when people are selected to do the work of finding the subject.

Character traits, habits, personality, trustworthiness, faithfulness, dependability and many other components of a person's makeup are explored and/or discovered when a committed individual or group seeks relentlessly to know the subject. If the person is identified then the predictive profiling can almost be relabeled, 'a sure thing'. In the world of people however there is possibility of change or deviation from trends or patterns. Man in general simply cannot be trusted and should not be. Our exercise below will consist of putting together two profiles.

Profile your best friend or a person who has influenced you most...then we will profile God. As an example I will profile my best friend of forty years. His name is Jerome.

Jerome has come from a home that fostered competition between several family members. He is partly a product of that environment.

Character traits—witty, calculating, intelligent. Not shifty. Who you see is what you get.

Habits—hard worker in own business and gardens. Habitually aids other people in need. Likes to be accurate in everything he says and does, thus, expects the same from others. Eats Organic as often as possible. Gets up early.

Personality—polite, enjoys good humor, not too outgoing but not withdrawn either. Does not like disrespect from anyone. Shows respect. His words are carefully chosen. Rarely does or says anything he has to apologize for. Can get angry at injustice.

Trustworthiness, faithfulness and dependability—. These are Jerome's shining points. He hates lies and does not lie. Jerome says something to someone else's benefit and lets nothing stop him from doing it. He is faithful to his words at all times. That also brings him the award for dependability. He received the trophy for assists in High School basketball. Jerome can be trusted, which is a big drawing point for him. People like to be in his company simply because of the absence of cynicism and ridicule

found in many others. He is a pleasant person to be near…
but don't cross him. (nice dogs fight the hardest)

Evidence that Jerome has been around can range from
kind words about him from others to, 'order' that has been
established in home and business. He is not a neat freak but
also is not disorderly. Needs a wife but his requirements are
currently very restricting and he knows it.

There are many other points to make about my friend but
this is only a gateway into discovering who God is, not a man.
Using the bible as a reference can produce much about the
Lord's aforementioned attributes. Because he is infinite/eternal,
the list can be refined and added to without contradiction.
When we are around a person who is the manifestation of
God's qualities there is that part of experience we can draw
from in our studies. There are many ways to know the Lord
better. Those numbers are infinite too. Let's set up an outline
to profile the Lord, thus the crux of this manual can also be:

HOW WELL DO I KNOW GOD?

For this final note section, I will start the profile of God and you can continue it. Remember, no one can finish it because the knowledge of God will not reach an end. I trust you have been blessed with more of Him during the time spent reading this manual. May you never cease in your hunger for the creator of all, Jesus Christ.

A baseline:

1. The Lord does not change.—Malachi 3:6
2. God is love.—1John 4:8
3. He disciplines those he loves.—Revelation 3:19
4. The Lord can get angry with an individual.—1Kings 11:9
5. The Lord can get angry with a nation.—1Kings 17:18
6. God blesses those who obey Him.—Genesis 22:18 Proverbs 10:6
7. The Lord curses…even a blessing.—Malachi 2:2
8. God can get jealous.—Exodus 20:5 One of his names is Jealous. Ex. 34:14
9. God is in control of all.—John 15:5
10. He is faithful.—Deuteronomy 7:9
11. God is fair.—Matthew 5:45b

12. The Lord is compassionate.—Psalms 86:15
13. The Lord is patient.—Romans 15:5
14. The Lord is merciful.—Deuteronomy 4:31
15. He creates evil.—Isaiah 45:7 (physical evil or calamity)
16. God destroys both the perfect and the wicked.—Job 9:22
17. God is sovereign.—Matthew 11:27
18. He is omnipotent (all powerful).—Revelation 19:6
19. The Lord is just, kind, righteous.—Jeremiah 9:24
20. The Lord knows everything. 1 Samuel 2:3
21. God gives.—Daniel 4:17 Psalms 104:27,28
22. God takes away.—Psalms 104:29
23. God is **the** healer.—Exodus 15:26
24. God is **the** provider.—Genesis 22:14 Hebrews 11 (emphasis v.40)
25. God rejoices.—Isaiah 62:5 Palms 104:31
26. God does not lie.—Titus 1:2 Hebrews 6:17-20
27. The Lord tests people.—Judges 7:4 1 Peter 4:12
28. The Lord distinguishes between us and Him.—Isaiah 55:8
29. His goodness endures continually.—Psalms 52:1
30. Other aspects of God's character.—Galatians 5:22,23

A) The above list can be divided into groups subjectively. Some are the ways God **thinks** while others are his **behavior**. Feel free to look up the provided scriptures and find others that further substantiate the claim of that particular aspect of God. Writing and going over your notes with others in a group will help you to learn.

B) Try to remember times, places, and circumstances in your own life when the Lord was working on your behalf and you at the time, did not see it that way. Have you changed at all in your views?

C) What aspects of the Lord have you observed working in other people's lives? Did their successes and failures help you in any way? (Keep the examples in the appropriate context)

EXHORTATION:

Before studying anything further in this manual it may be helpful to give you, the reader a note about the aforementioned material.

It is reasonable to assume that significant time and study went into the work. However, I have been humbled by the fact that even the Strong's Concordance expresses 35 years labor with more than 100 colleagues of Dr. Strong and still cannot claim 100% accuracy. For myself, it took 8 years and 128 pages of notes condensed down to 50 pages, reduced to 28 pages and then almost none of the material I saved to write was used. Less than one and a half pages of those original revelations were applicable. I have discovered that God is moving into the 'now' aspect of himself. There has been a reduction of leaning on 'what was' and into 'face to face' with Him all the time. A fraction of a second ago can possibly become stale.

My original hope was to get some script of eternal value into my writings and pray that there would be open hearts to the Lord to discern truth and live by it. Regardless of my intentions, any and all truth written should be scrutinized by such discerning hearts and resulting in subsequent growth (relationship) toward the Lord. He died for us and his life continues to stream from heaven above to the prepared hearts he has chosen. If you have heard his call to "come" please answer with a resounding "yes" and let Him be your, "all in all". It is then you will discover any aberrations in pen and ink will be handled with wisdom.

Chapter studies: Please use paper and pen by yourself and/ or with other people for potential discussions. Remember, there are an infinite number of ways the Lord may use all of us in aiding the progression of your individual relationship with Him.

FAITH

Write down and discuss examples of when the faith you did have was tested.

Did you receive more faith as a result?

Did you rebel and delay what God may have wanted to get to get you?

Were other people affected by your response to the Lord's approach to you?

Have the examples of others in your life helped you in the faith? If so how?

What famous stories of faith in the bible have been used by God to teach you about faith?

Are there examples in scripture that are now being brought alive to you by the Lord which once may not have meant much on the topic of faith?

What are my responsibilities to God in this area called Faith?

PROVISION

Have you known with your mind that God gives and takes away but have faltered when he really takes away?

What examples can you give that the Lord gave, threatened to take away but let you keep and then you succeeded in being faithful by the newfound revelation?

As a result, do you now have a greater fear or reverence of the Lord?

Have the experiences of others in scripture helped you in this area of Provision?

Have the experiences of others currently given you provision from the Lord?

Give examples of individuals or groups of people anywhere in the world, not just the people you may have been exposed to locally. Like scriptures themselves, other people's lives are meant very often to be a part of God's teachings for us.

What are my responsibilities to God on the subject of Works?

WORKS

Do I have a better understanding of what works really means?

Do I see more and more the works of God?

Is the revelation of God increasing in my life as a result?

Do I construe that God is the God of works? I am a vessel he pours His works through?

Are the things I say and do a voice and hand of the Lord? If not...why? If so, when and how did I discover that principle? What are my responsibilities to God with regard to "works".

A PRAYER

Lord, may you find us bent toward you like a flower toward the sun. Forgive us our sins and bring us back to the place you chose for us, oh, so long ago. Draw us nearer and may you be blessed by our choosing of you. Thank you for mercy, grace, and love when we didn't deserve it. Accept us now into the palm of your hand as a broken vessel to honor, not of dishonor, and may we reign with you forever and ever.

Written by Ronald w. knott 2010

Would you like to see your manuscript become a book?

If you are interested in becoming a PublishAmerica author, please submit your manuscript for possible publication to us at:

acquisitions@publishamerica.com

You may also mail in your manuscript to:

**PublishAmerica
PO Box 151
Frederick, MD 21705**

We also offer free graphics for Children's Picture Books!

---

www.publishamerica.com